REVISION GUIDE

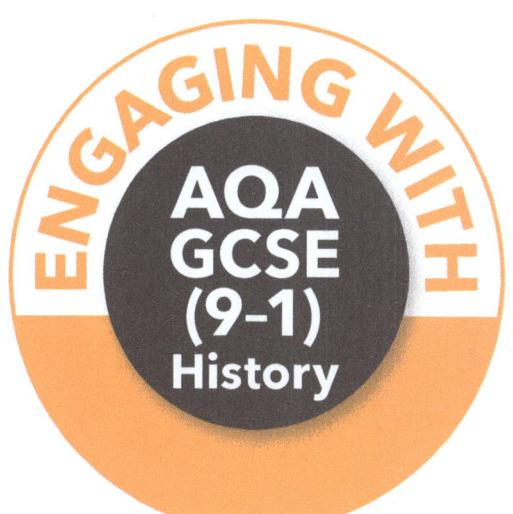

ENGAGING WITH AQA GCSE (9–1) History

GERMANY 1890–1945 DEMOCRACY AND DICTATORSHIP

PERIOD STUDY

DALE BANHAM

The Publishers would like to thank the following for permission to reproduce copyright material.

Photo credits

p.11 © Bettman/Corbis via Getty Images; **p.23** © Everett Collection Inc / Alamy Stock Photo; **p.39**t © Shawshots / Alamy Stock Photo, c © Image Bank / Alamy Stock Photo, b © Realimage / Alamy Stock Photo

Every effort has been made to trace all copyright holders, but if any have been inadvertently overlooked, the Publishers will be pleased to make the necessary arrangements at the first opportunity.

Although every effort has been made to ensure that website addresses are correct at time of going to press, Hodder Education cannot be held responsible for the content of any website mentioned in this book. It is sometimes possible to find a relocated web page by typing in the address of the home page for a website in the URL window of your browser.

Hachette UK's policy is to use papers that are natural, renewable and recyclable products and made from wood grown in well-managed forests and other controlled sources. The logging and manufacturing processes are expected to conform to the environmental regulations of the country of origin.

Orders: please contact Hachette UK Distribution, Hely Hutchinson Centre, Milton Road, Didcot, Oxfordshire, OX11 7HH. Telephone: +44 (0)1235 827827. Email education@hachette.co.uk Lines are open from 9 a.m. to 5 p.m., Monday to Friday. You can also order through our website: www.hoddereducation.co.uk

ISBN: 978 1 3983 8524 5

© Dale Banham 2023

First published in 2023 by
Hodder Education,
An Hachette UK Company
Carmelite House
50 Victoria Embankment
London EC4Y 0DZ

www.hoddereducation.co.uk

The authorised representative in the EEA is Hachette Ireland, 8 Castlecourt Centre, Dublin 15, D15 XTP3, Ireland (email: info@hbgi.ie)

Impression number   10 9 8 7 6 5 4 3 2

Year   2027 2026 2025 2024

All rights reserved. Apart from any use permitted under UK copyright law, no part of this publication may be reproduced or transmitted in any form or by any means, electronic or mechanical, including photocopying and recording, or held within any information storage and retrieval system, without permission in writing from the publisher or under licence from the Copyright Licensing Agency Limited. Further details of such licences (for reprographic reproduction) may be obtained from the Copyright Licensing Agency Limited, www.cla.co.uk

Cover photo © Pictorial Press Ltd / Alamy Stock Photo

Illustrations by Aptara, Inc.

Typeset in India by Aptara, Inc.

Printed in the UK

A catalogue record for this title is available from the British Library.

CONTENTS

Introduction: How to prepare for the exam — 4

Part 1: Germany and the growth of democracy, 1890–1929

Core content 1.1: Kaiser Wilhelm and the difficulties of ruling Germany — 8

Core content 1.2: The impact of the First World War — 10

Core content 1.3: Weimar democracy – political change and unrest (1919–23) — 12

Core content 1.4: Weimar democracy – the extent of recovery during the Stresemann era (1924–29) — 14

Apply: Exam practice — 16

Part 2: Germany and the Depression, 1929–34

Core content 2.1: The impact of the Depression and the growth in support for the Nazi Party — 22

Apply: Exam practice — 24

Core content 2.2: The failure of Weimar democracy — 26

Core content 2.3: The establishment of Hitler's dictatorship — 28

Apply: Exam practice — 30

Part 3: The experiences of Germans under the Nazis, 1933–45

Core content 3.1: Economic changes — 34

Core content 3.2: Nazi social policy and practice – the impact on women and young people — 36

Core content 3.3: Nazi social policy and practice – religion and racial persecution — 38

Core content 3.4: How Hitler kept control — 40

Core content 3.5: Opposition and resistance — 42

Apply: Exam practice — 44

Glossary — 48

How this book helps you revise and improve your grades

As you can see from this contents page, the book matches the exam specification and is divided into three time periods. You have already covered these with your teacher so each chapter starts with a **knowledge test** so that you can find out how much you can remember about each time period and plan a revision programme where you close gaps in your knowledge.

The **core content** pages will provide the answers to the questions you struggled with. These are designed in the style of flashcards so that you don't have to make your own and you can spend more time re-testing yourself and practising exam questions.

The book also shows you how to apply your knowledge to answer exam questions. Just knowing lots of information is not enough. The **Apply: Exam practice** pages will show you what to do with that knowledge so that you gain a high grade.

Introduction: How to prepare for the exam

Your exam: What is assessed and how

Your AQA GCSE (9–1) History course is made up of four different studies. These are assessed in two exam papers.

Paper 1: Understanding the modern world (2 hours)	Paper 2: Shaping the nation (2 hours)
Section A: Period study	**Section A: Thematic study**
This focuses on key developments in a country's history over at least a 50-year period.	This looks at key developments in Britain over a long period of time (at least 800 years).
Section B: Wider world depth study	**Section B: British depth study**
This focuses on international conflict and tension over a period of 20–25 years.	This focuses on a period of British history over a short period of time (under 40 years).

This book prepares you for Section A of Paper 1 – **Germany 1890–1945: Democracy and Dictatorship**. The table below shows you how the period study will be examined.

	Type of question	Guidance	Marks	Timing	Advice and practice
Questions 1–3 will be based on two written interpretations. The authors of these interpretations will have been present when an event took place, but they will have written their interpretation of the event a number of years later.					
1	How do interpretations differ?	The focus is on identifying differences in the content or attitude or viewpoint of the two interpretations.	4	5 minutes	Pages 24 and 44
2	Why do interpretations differ?	In order to explain these differences, you will need to focus on the provenance (authorship) of each interpretation: • Who wrote it? • Where did they get their information from? • When was it written? • Why was it written?	4	5 minutes	Pages 24 and 44
3	Which interpretation is the most convincing?	You will need to use your knowledge and understanding of the period to judge which interpretation is the most convincing. For each interpretation, focus on how far it matches your contextual knowledge of the period – is it typical of what was happening at the time?	8	10 minutes	Pages 25 and 44
Questions 4–6 will focus on second order concepts such as causation or change.					
4	Describe	You will need to describe two key features or characteristics of a topic you have studied.	4	5 minutes	Pages 16 and 46
5	Explain	You will need to explain in what ways a group or development was affected by something.	8	10 minutes	Pages 16 and 46
6	Evaluate	You must write an essay weighing up two bullet points. They might be causes (e.g. which played the most important role in causing a development) or consequences (e.g. which was affected most by …).	12	15 minutes	Pages 18, 30 and 47

Your exam: The key steps to success

This book uses the latest research into effective revision strategies to help you remember the core content. The specification is divided into three time periods so follow the structure of the book and break your revision down into three parts. For each time period, follow the steps below. They will help you revise more effectively – saving you time and boosting your grade

Step 1: Test your knowledge and understanding

The specification is divided into three time periods:
- Germany and the growth of democracy, 1890–1929
- Germany and the Depression, 1929–34
- The experiences of Germans under the Nazis, 1933–45

You have already covered these periods with your teacher so start by testing yourself – how much can you remember about each time period? Each part of this book starts with a **Knowledge test** that covers the key content for that period.

Testing yourself is a great way to start your revision as it **boosts memory**.

When you test yourself your memory of that information gets significantly stronger. Our brains are also hard-wired to learn from our mistakes.

It helps you understand what you already know and what you don't know.

Step 2: Identify gaps in your knowledge and understanding

You will be able to check your answers to the knowledge test. Page references are provided so you can identify gaps in your knowledge.

You will be able to plan an efficient revision programme. Your time is precious, so you need to make sure that you focus on revising your weaker topics. Too many students spend too much time revising topics they already know very well.

Step 3: Close the gaps in your knowledge and understanding

The **core content** pages in this book will help you improve your knowledge and understanding of your weaker topics. Each of the three periods is divided into core content pages that closely match the exam specification. This makes revising a topic a manageable task.

At the top of the page, a checklist of the core content from the specification is provided so that you can rate your understanding and identify topics that you need to focus on.

Memory aids are provided to help you remember key events or developments. They use images or diagrams, but very few words. Most people remember better if something is summarised with both text and images.

Step 4: Apply your knowledge and understanding to exam questions

When you feel confident with the content for each time period, use the **Apply: Exam practice** pages in the book to gain a strong understanding of how to approach each of the six exam questions (see page 4).

Our practice questions are like the questions you will be asked in the exam. You can get past papers from your teacher or from the AQA website. We provide **Exam Tips** for each question type – showing you how to approach it and improve your grades.

Step 5: Review your exam answers and respond to feedback

This book provides model answers that highlight the key features of high-quality written work. The exam practice pages also provide **Exam Tips** that you can use to review your own work.

Use the advice provided as a checklist to reflect on your own answers. Take responsibility for your own learning. Before you ask your teacher for any additional feedback, make sure your answer is the best it can be.

Part 1 Germany and the growth of democracy, 1890–1929

Knowledge test: How much do you know about Germany between 1890 and 1929?

It may seem strange starting your revision with a knowledge test but remember this is the best way to boost your memory and it will help you identify gaps in your knowledge. Don't worry if you cannot answer all the questions or if you make mistakes. You can use the core content pages to check your answers and fill in the gaps in your knowledge.

> **Revision Tip**
>
> When you have finished all the **Recall challenges**, use the page references in blue to check your answers. If you have made a mistake, **use a different colour pen to write in the correct answer**.

Recall challenges

1: Do you know the key terms?

Match each key term with its correct definition or description.

Key term	Definition
Republic	An organisation made up of armed ex-soldiers
Constitution	Organisations set up to protect and improve the rights of workers
Prussian militarism	The main left-wing political party in Germany. It wanted resources to be shared out equally and better pay and conditions for workers
Reparations	Admiration for the army (Prussia was the largest state in Germany)
The Reichstag	A belief in a society where all resources are shared out equally and there is no private property
Trade unions	The rich, land-owning class in Germany (most fully supported the Kaiser)
Putsch	A system where the government is chosen by the people
Communists	The set of rules for how a country should be governed
Junkers	Compensation that Germany had to pay for the damage caused in the First World War
Democracy	A state that has an elected leader rather than a hereditary ruler (e.g. a monarch)
Social Democratic Party	An armed uprising aimed at taking over the government
Freikorps	The German parliament – made up of members who were elected by voters

2: Do you know the key individuals?

Match each individual with the correct description.

Key individual	Description
Kaiser Wilhelm	Played a leading role in the government of the Weimar Republic between 1923 and 1929 (firstly as Chancellor, then as Foreign Minister)
Admiral von Tirpitz	Leader of the Nazi Party who led a putsch against the Weimar government in Munich in 1923
Rosa Luxemburg	A Social Democrat who became the first President of the Weimar Republic
General Ludendorff	Believed that Germany needed to increase the size of its navy so that it could build an overseas empire
Adolf Hitler	Leader of the Spartacists who led an uprising against the government in 1919
Gustav Stresemann	A popular First World War hero who was involved in both the Kapp Putsch and the Munich Putsch
Fredrich Ebert	The German king (monarch) who ruled from 1888 to 1918

3: Do you know the key events and developments?

Task

Answer as many of the questions below as you can.
- Mark your work using the page numbers provided. A total of 60 marks are available.
- Use the quiz to identify areas you need to revise in detail.

List two aims of Kaiser Wilhelm II.	List three factors that could help the Kaiser achieve his aims.	List three difficulties the Kaiser faced in ruling Germany.	See pages 8–9 for the answers	Mark out of 15
List two examples of the Kaiser introducing social reforms.	List two examples of the Kaiser using threats and punishments against his opponents.	List three reasons why the Naval Laws were introduced.		
List three ways in which life changed for the German people during the First World War.	List four key terms of the Treaty of Versailles.	List three problems that Germany faced in the post-war period (1919–23).	See pages 10–11 for the answers	Mark out of 15
List two groups of people who suffered from hyperinflation.	List two groups of people who gained from hyperinflation.	How many marks was one dollar worth in November 1923?		
List two features of the Weimar Constitution that made it more democratic.	List two problems of the Weimar Constitution.	List three political groups that supported the Weimar Republic.	See pages 12–13 for the answers	Mark out of 15
List three political groups that opposed the Weimar Republic.	List three examples of attempts to overthrow the Weimar government.	List two reasons why the Munich Putsch failed.		
List three international agreements that helped Germany recover during the Stresemann era.	List two economic developments that helped Germany recover during the Stresemann era.	List two problems that remained during the Stresemann era.	See pages 14–15 for the answers	Mark out of 15
List three examples of how Weimar culture became more open and challenged traditional values.	List three examples of how Weimar culture contained strong political messages.	List two reasons why some people were angered by Weimar culture.		

Core content 1.1: Kaiser Wilhelm and the difficulties of ruling Germany

Exam specification checklist for this topic
- The growth of parliamentary government
- The influence of Prussian militarism
- Industrialisation
- Social reform and the growth of socialism
- The domestic importance of the Navy Laws

Revision task
Use the flashcards on pages 8–9 to improve your knowledge and understanding of these topics. Test yourself by trying to answer the key questions with the bullet point answers covered up. Make a note of the topics you struggle to remember – you can spend more time on them later in your revision programme.

Key question 1: What did Kaiser Wilhelm II want to achieve?

Aim 1: Control the political system
- He believed in the divine right of kings – the belief that a king's right to rule came directly from God.
- He wanted to make the big political decisions and he had little respect for the Reichstag (the German parliament).

Aim 2: Make Germany a leading world power
- He believed that Germany needed and deserved a large overseas empire, like those of France and Britain.
- This meant that Germany needed to build up its army and navy.

Key question 2: What factors helped Kaiser Wilhelm II?

- **Industrialisation** – Between 1890 and 1910 the German population increased from 49 million to 65 million. Many people moved from farms in the countryside to work in industries in the towns and cities. This led to a growing German economy. Germany produced one third of the world's electrical goods and had very successful engineering, chemical and steel industries. A strong, industrial economy made it easier for the Kaiser to build up a strong army and navy.

- **Prussian militarism** – Prussia was the most important state in Germany; it contained two thirds of the population. Prussia was very proud of its military strength and history. This meant that many people in Germany admired the army and supported the Kaiser's plans to build up the strength of the German military.

- **The Junkers** – These powerful landowners held key positions in the army and dominated politics. They supported the Kaiser's plans to build an overseas empire and they did not want to see democracy increasing in Germany. Like the Kaiser, they wanted to keep power for themselves.

Key question 3: What difficulties did Kaiser Wilhelm II face?

- **S = Socialism** was increasing – Socialists wanted major reforms to improve living and working conditions for ordinary people. They also wanted to see less of a gap between the rich and the poor. Most socialists joined the Social Democratic Party. By 1912, it was the largest party in the Reichstag.

- **T = Trade unions** were growing as a result of industrialisation. Many workers who found jobs in the factories in the towns and cities joined trade unions, which demanded better pay and working conditions for their members. By 1914, 3 million workers had joined trade unions, which could organise strikes (when workers refused to work) and damage the economy.
- **O = Opposition** to the Kaiser was growing in the Reichstag and this created problems for the Kaiser as he needed the support of the Reichstag to pass laws and agree on taxes. Left-wing parties such as the Social Democrats wanted change and protested when the Kaiser did not introduce the reforms they wanted.
- **P = Parties** in the Reichstag wanted to see parliamentary government. Liberals and Social Democrats wanted to create a more democratic way of ruling Germany in which the Kaiser had far less power.

Key question 4: How did the Kaiser respond to the growth of socialism and demands for social reform?

The Kaiser responded to the growing demands of the Socialists with an inconsistent mix of **reforms** (designed to please working people) and **repression** (attempts to crush the socialists through threats and intimidation).

Sunday working banned

Reform … Wilhelm's first chancellor, **Caprivi**, introduced some social reforms in the 1890s. Sunday working was banned. Children under 13 years of age could no longer be employed. Food prices were lowered.

Workers' benefits extended

Reform … In 1900, **Bulow** became Chancellor. He introduced some social reforms. For example, workers' pension and insurance benefits were extended. However, workers suffered when food prices rose. Bulow was unable to stop prices rising and he lost the support of the socialists in the Reichstag.

Social Democrat leaders on trial

Repression … However, by 1894, Wilhelm felt threatened by the growing strength of the Social Democrats. He decided to take a strong line against them. Their offices were attacked and leaders were put on trial. In 1898, Wilhelm made a speech saying that any worker who went on strike and refused to work should be put in prison. When the Reichstag opposed this, Wilhelm suggested that Social Democrat members should be dragged out of the Reichstag and gunned down by troops!

REFORM ←——————————————————→ REPRESSION

Key question 5: Why were the Naval Laws introduced and what consequences did they have?

Causes

- **The Kaiser's aims** – He was determined to build an overseas empire for Germany. He thought that this would provide the resources and markets Germany needed to grow its economy and play a leading role in world politics.
- **The role of Admiral von Tirpitz** (the Secretary of State for the Navy) – He agreed with the Kaiser and argued that a strong German navy would frighten the British and mean that they would not try to stop Germany building an overseas empire.
- **The Navy League** – Tirpitz helped to set this up, in order to try to win popular support for his plans to expand the navy. Tirpitz knew he needed the support of the Reichstag for his plans. The Navy League helped to persuade members of the Reichstag to vote for two Naval Laws.

Consequences

- **The First Naval Law (1898)** – Seven new battleships were to be built over the next three years.
- **The Second Naval Law (1900)** – Doubled the size of the German navy.
- **Taxes increased** – Most Germans supported the expansion of the navy but it significantly increased government debt and led to increased taxes.
- **International tension increased** – France, Russia and Britain felt threatened by the expansion of the German navy. Britain built up the size of its navy and formed an alliance with France and Russia (the Triple Entente).

Core content 1.2: The impact of the First World War

Exam specification checklist for this topic
- War weariness
- Economic problems
- Defeat and the end of the monarchy
- Post-war problems including reparations, the occupation of the Ruhr and hyperinflation

Revision task
Use the flashcards on pages 10–11 to improve your knowledge and understanding of these topics. Test yourself by trying to answer the key questions with the bullet point answers covered up. Make a note of the topics you struggle to remember – you can spend more time on them later in your revision programme.

Key question 1: In what ways did life change for people living in Germany during the First World War?

- **Economic problems** – Factories lost workers as many men signed up to fight in the war. By 1918, German industry was producing only two thirds of what it had before the war. The German government started to run out of money and supplies.
- **War weariness** – There were serious food and fuel shortages: many German people were forced to survive on bread and turnips. Wages were kept low, even though some factory owners were making huge profits from supplying goods for the war effort. As the war dragged on, this led to a drop in morale as well as protests and strikes. There were uprisings led by soldiers and workers in many German ports and cities.
- **The end of the monarchy** – When he realised that Germany faced defeat in the war, the Kaiser abdicated (resigned). Germany became a republic and a new democratic government was set up. Fredrich Ebert (leader of the Social Democrats) was elected leader of the Weimar Republic.
- **Defeat and the 'stab in the back' myth** – The new Weimar government had little choice but to surrender to the Allies (France, Britain, Russia, Italy, Japan and the USA) and sign an armistice (in November 1918) that ended the war. This angered some soldiers and civilians who felt that Germany should have continued to fight on. They believed that Germany had been 'stabbed in the back' by weak politicians and they called the leaders of the Weimar government who agreed to the armistice the 'November criminals'.

Key question 2: Why did the German people hate the Treaty of Versailles?

An acronym such as **LAMB** can help you remember the four main terms of the treaty. Combine your acronym with a memorable image and story. Think of the Germans being like lambs to the slaughter – after the war ended, Germany had no say in the treaty and other countries were keen to punish Germany.

- **Land** – Germany lost 10 per cent of its land, which contained 13 per cent of its population and important raw materials. It lost all of its colonies and 26 per cent of its coal resources.
- **Army** – The German army was reduced to 100,000 men. It was only allowed six battleships. It was not allowed an air force, tanks or submarines.
- **Money** – Germany had to pay reparations – compensation for the damage that had been caused in the war. Most of the money would go to France, Belgium and Britain. At Versailles, the Allies could not agree on the amount. In 1921, the Allies agreed that Germany should pay £6600 million in gold.
- **Blame** – In clause 231 of the treaty (the war guilt clause), Germany was blamed for causing the First World War.

Key question 3: What problems did Germany face during the post-war period (1919–23)?

Reparations
- In 1922, Germany announced that it could not afford to pay reparations for the next three years.
- France did not believe this and was determined to make Germany pay.

This led to …

The occupation of the Ruhr
- In 1923, 60,000 French and Belgian soldiers marched into the Ruhr (an important industrial area of Germany).
- They occupied the area for ten months, seizing control of all the mines, factories and railways. They set up machine-gun posts in the street and took what was owed to them in reparations in the form of goods and raw materials.
- The German government told workers not to co-operate with the French and Belgian soldiers. All workers went on strike. The policy was known as **passive resistance**. It was meant to be a non-violent protest but 140 Germans were killed in clashes with the soldiers.
- The invasion of the Ruhr added to Germany's economic problems. No money was coming in from one of the most important industrial areas and the workers who had gone on strike needed money to support their families. The government responded by printing more money to pay the workers but …

This led to …

Hyperinflation
- The more money the government printed, the less it was worth. People started to lose confidence in the value of the German mark. Prices rose at an incredible rate (this is known as hyperinflation).
- By November 1923, an egg cost 80 million marks and a glass of beer cost 150 million marks. One US dollar was worth 200 billion marks (the photo on the left was taken to show how many German marks were equal to one US dollar).

Key question 4: In what ways were the lives of German people affected by hyperinflation?

In the short-term, many people lost out
- Many workers found that their wages could not keep up with prices – they could not afford to buy the goods they needed.
- There were food shortages because farmers did not want to sell food for worthless money. As a result, there were deaths from starvation.
- Older people who were receiving a pension found that their monthly income could not even buy a cup of coffee.
- Middle-class people with savings that could have bought a house before hyperinflation found that these saving would only now buy a loaf of bread. Millions lost their savings. Of course, those in poverty suffered even more.
- Poverty and crime increased.

However, some people gained
- People in debt found that they could pay off their loans. Business owners found it a lot easier to pay back the money they had borrowed.
- The profit made by big businesses increased because the prices they could sell their goods for increased at a faster rate than the wages they had to pay their workers.

In the long-term, the Weimar Republic was seriously weakened
- People blamed the Weimar government for the problems that were caused by hyperinflation. Ordinary Germans seemed to have lost out, while business owners made big profits.
- People lost confidence in the new Weimar Republic and some people turned against the democratic political parties that supported the Weimar government. Support for extremist parties such as the Nazis and the Communists increased.

Core content 1.3: Weimar democracy – political change and unrest (1919–23)

Exam specification checklist for this topic

- The Weimar Constitution
- The Spartacist uprising
- The Kapp Putsch
- The Munich Putsch

Revision task

Use the flashcards on pages 12–13 to improve your knowledge and understanding of these topics. Test yourself by trying to answer the key questions with the bullet point answers covered up. Make a note of the topics you struggle to remember – you can spend more time on them later in your revision programme.

Key question 1: What were the strengths of the Weimar Constitution?

During 1919, a new set of rules was drawn up for how Germany should be governed. The Weimar Constitution was one of the most democratic systems of government in the world, but it also had some features that caused political problems.

Strengths

- All men and women over the age of 20 could vote for the President (every seven years) and members of the Reichstag (every four years).
- Members of the Reichstag were elected every four years, through a system called proportional representation (if a party got 45 per cent of the vote, it got 45 per cent of the seats in the Reichstag). This gave smaller political parties a chance to have a say in the government.
- Members of the Reichstag voted on new laws. To pass laws, the Chancellor (like a prime minister) needed the support of more than half of the Reichstag.
- All adults had equal rights and the right of free speech.
- Most people in Germany supported the new constitution and wanted democracy to succeed.

Key question 2: What were the weaknesses of the Weimar Constitution?

Weaknesses

- The President of Germany had a lot of power. He chose the Chancellor from the Reichstag. He controlled the armed forces and, in an emergency, he could make laws without going through the Reichstag.
- During the 1920s, no political party gained more than 50 per cent of the vote. This meant that political parties had to join together to form **coalition governments**. This caused problems if the parties could not agree on policies and changes to the law.
- Some political parties (see below) did not support the new system of government. Extremist groups, on both the left and right wing, wanted to overthrow the Weimar government. This led to political violence (see Key question 3).

Key question 3: Who supported the Weimar Republic?

- The **Social Democrats** were the main party involved in setting up the Weimar Republic. They had lots of support – mainly from the working class. They wanted to introduce reforms to help workers and create a more equal distribution of wealth.
- The **Centre Party**'s main aim was to protect the interests of the Catholic Church.
- The **Democratic Party** was mainly supported by the middle class.
- The **People's Party**'s main support came from the middle class and industrialists.

Key question 4: Who opposed the Weimar Republic?

- The **Communist Party** believed that it should run the country on behalf of the workers.
  It wanted the government to run all farms and businesses for the benefit of all people.
  It believed that wealth should be shared out equally and that there should be no private property.

- The **Nazi Party** and the **German National Party** believed that Germany should have one strong leader. They wanted to ignore the Treaty of Versailles and build a strong army.
  The German National Party wanted Germany to return to what it was like before 1918, when it was ruled by a monarch.

Task
Which political group represented the biggest threat to the Weimar Republic?

Use the table below to evaluate the risk posed by the each of the three examples of political unrest. Give the event a danger rating out of 10 and use the criteria below to explain why you have given it this rating.

Criteria:
- How big was their support?
- How well organised were they?
- How close did they come to success?

Key question 5: How big was the threat from political unrest between 1919 and 1923?

Spartacist uprising (1919)

Who supported it?	The Spartacist League was a communist group led by Rosa Luxemburg and Karl Liebknecht.
Why did they rebel?	It did not believe the new government would do enough to improve workers' lives. It wanted a full-scale communist revolution (like the Russian Revolution of 1917).
What happened?	It took over the government's newspaper and telegraph headquarters in Berlin. The leaders hoped protesters would join them and take over other buildings, but this did not happen. Poor planning meant that the Spartacists did not get support from other left-wing groups.
What was the result?	The government used the army and units of the Freikorps (armed ex-soldiers) to stop the uprising and quickly regain control. Over 100 Spartacists were killed, including Luxemburg and Liebknecht.

Kapp Putsch (1920)

Who supported it?	Freikorps units led by Wolfgang Kapp. Around 12,000 Freikorps marched to Berlin.
Why did they rebel?	The Weimar government had made it clear that it wanted to disband the Freikorps. The Freikorps wanted to set up a new right-wing government, led by Kapp.
What happened?	The Weimar government was forced to leave Berlin. It asked the trade unions and workers to go on strike and refuse to co-operate with Kapp and the Freikorps.
What was the result?	The Freikorps failed to win popular support. The strikes and protests made it impossible for Kapp to rule. After four days, Kapp fled from Berlin and the Weimar government returned.

Munich Putsch (1923)

Who supported it?	The putsch was planned by General Ludendorff (a popular war hero) and Adolf Hitler (leader of the Nazi Party). At the time, the Nazi Party had 55,000 members and its own private army (the SA).
Why did they rebel?	The Nazi Party believed that democracy led to weak government. It thought there should be one political party, with one leader. It planned to take over the government and set up Ludendorff as the leader of Germany.
What happened?	Hitler believed that Gustav von Kahr (the right-wing prime minister of Bavaria) and Otto von Lossow (the head of the Bavarian army) would support his putsch. Hitler and 600 of his SA burst into a meeting in a beer hall in Munich and forced Kahr and Lossow, at gun point, to say that they would support a march on Berlin.
What was the result?	After they were released by Hitler, Kahr and Lossow decided not to oppose the putsch. When 2000 armed Nazis marched towards a military base in Munich they were stopped by armed police and Bavarian soldiers. Fourteen Nazis were killed, and Hitler and Ludendorff were arrested.

Core content 1.4: Weimar democracy – the extent of recovery during the Stresemann era (1924–29)

Exam specification checklist for this topic

- Economic developments including the new currency
- The Dawes Plan and the Young Plan
- The impact of international agreements on recovery
- Weimar culture

Revision task

Use the flashcards on pages 14–15 to improve your knowledge and understanding of these topics. Test yourself by trying to answer the key questions with the bullet point answers covered up. Make a note of the topics you struggle to remember – you can spend more time on them later in your revision programme.

Key question 1: What developments helped the Weimar Republic to recover during the Stresemann era?

Good relations with other countries
Occupation of the Ruhr ended
Loans from USA
Dawes Plan
Economy improved
New currency introduced

International agreements

Stresemann developed **good relations with other countries**. He signed important international agreements that built trust and helped to bring in loans and investment from other countries, particularly the United States. His actions also helped to persuade the Allies to reduce reparation payments and give Germany longer to pay them.

Examples of international agreements:

- 1923 Stresemann called off passive resistance in the Ruhr and promised to restart reparation payments. As a result, the **French left the Ruhr**.
- 1924 The **Dawes Plan** gave Germany longer to pay reparations.
- 1925 Stresemann signed the **Locarno Pact** with Britain, France, Belgium and Italy. They promised not to invade each other and to respect the borders established in the Treaty of Versailles.
- 1926 Germany joined the League of Nations.
- 1928 Germany and 64 other countries signed the **Kellogg–Briand Pact**. It agreed that international disputes should be settled by 'peaceful means'.
- 1929 The **Young Plan** lowered reparations from £6600 million to less than £2000 million.

Economic developments

- Stresemann helped to end hyperinflation by introducing a **new currency** called the Rentenmark. It was quickly accepted by the German people and inflation was brought under control.
- Stresemann organised loans from the USA as part of the **Dawes Plan** (1924). These loans gave a massive boost to the German economy. Loans were made to German firms and exports increased. Many US firms set up businesses in Germany. By 1928, Germany was the world's second strongest economy (behind the USA).
- The Weimar government also used the loans to improve housing and build new schools, hospitals and roads.

Key question 2: What were the key features of Weimar culture?

The 3 Cs of Weimar culture
- **C**ensorship restrictions removed
- **C**hallenged traditional values
- **C**riticised the government

Key feature of Weimar culture	Examples
During the era of Kaiser Wilhelm II, there had been strict **censorship** in Germany. During the time of the Weimar Republic, many restrictions were removed. There was an atmosphere of freedom and experimentation.	• **Clubs and cabaret** – Going to clubs became a major pastime for men and women. Berlin became famous for its cabaret clubs, transvestite balls, naked dancing and nightclubs.
Weimar culture **challenged** traditional values and styles that had existed during the time of Kaiser Wilhelm II.	• **Cinema** – Films became very popular and directors like Fritz Lang produced new styles such as vampire horror movies. Actresses like Marlene Dietrich played strong and glamorous female characters. • **Architecture** – Bauhaus architects made use of modern materials like steel and glass to design new styles of houses and shops.
Some forms of Weimar culture openly **criticised** the government and German society.	• **Art** – Otto Dix produced paintings that highlighted the inequalities that existed between rich and poor people in Germany. • **Literature** – Writers such as Erich Remarque produced novels with strong anti-war messages. His popular book, *All Quiet on the Western Front,* was a powerful description of the horrors of the First World War. • **Theatre** – Directors such as Bertolt Brecht produced plays about ordinary people. Brecht was a communist and wanted to show that the lives of ordinary people were just as suitable subjects for operas as stories of heroes and gods.

Key question 3: Why did Weimar culture annoy some German people?

- Some Germans were shocked by the club scene in Berlin. They thought that Weimar culture represented a moral decline and things had gone too far. The Wandervogel movement argued for a return to simple, traditional, family values.
- Both Catholic and Protestant Churches spoke out against what they saw as a decline in public morals and Christian values.
- Some Germans thought that the work of artists and writers that criticised the government and the war was unpatriotic.
- Some Germans did not like the new styles of art and architecture. They wanted to keep the traditional buildings of the Kaiser's Germany and preferred paintings and sculptures to show heroic-looking Germans and military figures.

Apply: Exam practice

Question 4: How to approach the describe question

Question 4 on the exam paper asks you to describe two key features or characteristics of a topic you have studied. Be careful not to spend too long on this question – aim for 5 minutes. Keep your answer very focused on the question and do not write more than one paragraph. Use the Exam Tips box to help you structure your answers to the practice questions below.

Tasks

1. Use the Exam Tips box to complete the first exam question below.
2. Now that you are aware of the structure, have a go at answering the second and third practice questions.

- **Describe two problems faced by Kaiser Wilhelm II's governments in ruling Germany up to 1914.** (4 marks)
- **Describe two problems for the German government caused by the occupation of the Ruhr in 1923.** (4 marks)
- **Describe two problems that the Weimar government faced as a result of hyperinflation.** (4 marks)

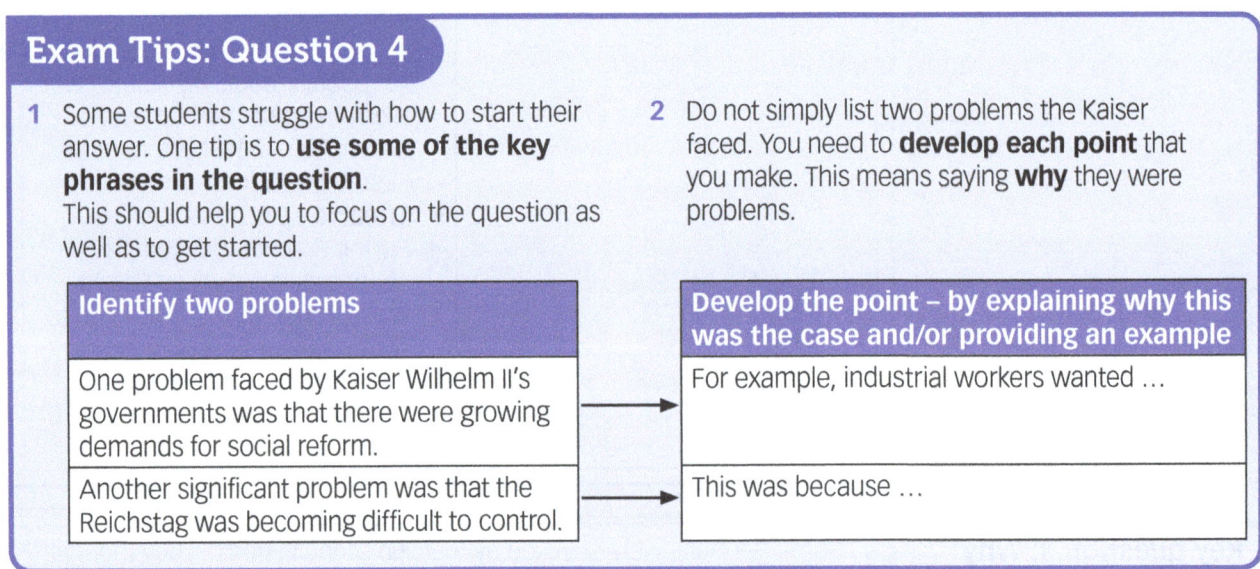

Exam Tips: Question 4

1. Some students struggle with how to start their answer. One tip is to **use some of the key phrases in the question**.
   This should help you to focus on the question as well as to get started.

2. Do not simply list two problems the Kaiser faced. You need to **develop each point** that you make. This means saying **why** they were problems.

Identify two problems	Develop the point – by explaining why this was the case and/or providing an example
One problem faced by Kaiser Wilhelm II's governments was that there were growing demands for social reform.	For example, industrial workers wanted …
Another significant problem was that the Reichstag was becoming difficult to control.	This was because …

Question 5: How to approach the explain question

Question 5 on the exam paper often focuses on the impact of an event or development on the lives of people living at the time. Aim to spend about 10 minutes on the question and to write two or three paragraphs. We have broken down the approach you should take into four steps. The 4Ds are very important as you can use these steps for Question 6 as well.

Tasks

1. Complete the practice question in the Exam tips box.

In what ways did life change for people living in Germany during the First World War? (8 marks)

2. Use the 4Ds approach for the two further exam practice questions at the bottom of page 17.

Exam Tips

Think before you write using the **4Ds**.

Step 1: Decode the question

Staying focused on the question is crucial. If you include information that is not relevant or write about the wrong topic you will waste time and not gain marks. Here's how to decode a question.

What are the command words? The question starts 'In what ways' (**plural**). You need to explain at least two and preferably three changes.

What is the conceptual focus? The historical concept is **change**. Describing what life was like during the war is not enough to get the higher-level marks. Focus on the changes that took place during the war. State what life was like at the start of the war and then explain how this changed during the war.

<u>In what ways</u> did <u>life</u> <u>change</u> for <u>people living in Germany during the First World War</u>? **(8 marks)**

What is the content focus? Focus on the lives of German people during the First World War. Mentioning problems after the war will waste time and not gain you marks.

How many marks are available? '8 marks' indicates that you should spend about 10 minutes on the question and write two or three paragraphs (one per change).

Step 2: Decide how to organise your answer before you start to write

Plan the focus for each paragraph. For this question, you could focus on economic changes in your first paragraph and political changes in your second paragraph. The example below shows how you can quickly plan your answer.

Paragraph 1: Economic changes
- Factories lose workers – production drops
- Food and fuel shortages

Paragraph 2: Political changes
- People turn against the war – uprisings – workers and soldiers
- Kaiser abdicates – new political system

Step 3: Develop your answer – as you write, explain and support the points you make

Do not simply list points. Develop your answer by:
- **Giving specific supporting examples** – for example: By 1918, German industry was producing only two-thirds of what it had been producing before the war.
- **Explaining the impact of the changes that took place** – for example: Food and fuel shortages led to war weariness and a drop in morale. This meant that strikes and political protests increased.

Step 4: Demonstrate complex thinking

For a top-level mark, you need to show that you are thinking in a complex way about the impact of the changes that occurred. You could add a short conclusion that shows a deeper understanding of history. For example:

- **Did everyone experience the same impact?** Do not give the impression that change affected everyone in the same way. In the case of this question, did the war have a negative impact on all Germans? Remember that some factory owners made large profits from the war by producing goods for the German army.
- **How fast did change occur?** Do not give the impression that you think all the changes happened immediately. It took time for the economic changes to lead to a drop in morale. Political change (in the form of strikes and uprisings) happened towards the end of the war.

Apply: further exam practice

In what ways were the lives of the German people affected by events in Germany between 1919 and 1923? **(8 marks)**

In what ways did the lives of the German people change during the Golden Twenties (1924–28)? **(8 marks)**

Question 6: How to approach the evaluate question

Question 6 on the exam paper asks you to evaluate the importance of two bullet points. For example, in the practice question below, you are being asked to evaluate which factor was the most important reason why the Weimar Republic was in danger between 1919 and 1923. There are 12 marks available, so it is worth planning your approach to this question. Aim to spend about 15 minutes on Question 6 and to write three paragraphs. We have broken down the approach you should take into four steps (the 4Ds from page 17).

Tasks

1. Complete the practice question in the Exam tips box below. Make notes so that you have a good plan before you write your answer.
2. Use the same process and planning model to answer the exam practice question on page 19.

Exam Tips

Which of the following was the most important reason why the Weimar Republic faced difficulties between 1919 and 1923?

- Economic problems
- Political unrest

(12 marks)

Think before you write using the **4Ds**.

Step 1: **Decode** the question

- Note the dates – make sure you focus on the time period stated in the question. You will waste time and gain no marks if you go beyond the date boundaries.
- Note the conceptual focus of the question. Here the focus is on causation – evaluating which of two causal factors was more important.

Step 2: **Decide** how to organise your answer

Plan your answer using three paragraphs. Aim to write one paragraph on each of the bullet points, then add a conclusion in which you reach your final judgement on which was more important. Look at the developments and events below. Which would you include in your answer and what paragraph would they go in? Complete the table that has been started for you.

- Place an **E** next to things that were economic problems between 1919 and 1923.
- Place a **P** next to things that are examples of political unrest between 1919 and 1923.
- Place an **X** next to things that would not go in your answer as they did not take place between 1919 and 1923.

Spartacist uprising	P	Occupation of the Ruhr	
Dawes Plan		Locarno Treaty	
Munich Putsch		Reparation payments	
Hyperinflation		Kapp Putsch	

Step 3: **Develop** your answer

Do not just produce a list of developments or events. For each one:
- Briefly explain why it happened.
- Briefly describe what happened – include specific details (see the statistics included in the model answer opposite).
- Explain the impact. Don't just say something was important – prove it was! Why did the development or event lead to problems for the Weimar Republic?

How to produce a developed answer

The example below shows you how to produce a developed explanation of the occupation of the Ruhr. Complete the planning table for hyperinflation.

Identify the event	**Explain** why it happened	**Describe** what happened	**Explain** the impact
The occupation of the Ruhr was an important economic problem.	French and Belgian troops invaded the Ruhr after Germany announced it could not afford to pay reparations.	In 1923, **60,000** troops marched into the Ruhr, an important industrial area in Germany. They occupied the area for **ten months**, taking what was owed to them in raw materials and goods. The German government told people in the Ruhr not to co-operate and all workers went on strike. A total of **140** Germans were killed in clashes with the troops.	The occupation of the Ruhr created severe economic problems. The German economy had been left in a weak position at the end of the war and the invasion meant that no money came in from one of its main industrial areas. Workers who went on strike needed money from the government to support their families. In addition, the occupation added to the anger and humiliation many Germans felt after the Treaty of Versailles.
Hyperinflation was another major economic problem.	This occurred when the government …	Prices rose at an incredible rate. For example, …	This had a serious impact on many groups of people in Germany. For example, …

Step 4: **Demonstrate** complex thinking

For a top-level mark, you need to show that you are thinking in a complex way about the impact of the developments and events that occurred. In your third paragraph, you should add a short conclusion that shows a deeper understanding of history.

Explain links between the causes

What is the relationship between the causes? Did economic problems lead to an increase in political unrest? For example, anger at the reparations and the humiliation that was felt after the occupation of the Ruhr led to growing discontent with the Weimar government. This led to groups such as the Nazis being able to build support and think that they would be able to overthrow the government.

Use criteria to explain your final judgement

Why are some causes more important than others? You could think about:
- What was the **scale** of the impact? How big was the problem? How many people were affected? For example, hyperinflation created problems for many different groups of people and the scale of the rises in prices was unprecedented.
- How **long-lasting** was the impact? Did certain events cause problems over a long period of time (for example, the ten-month occupation of the Ruhr)? Did other events (for example, political unrest like the Munich Putsch) only represent a temporary danger?

Apply: Further exam practice

Which of the following was the most important reason why the Weimar Republic was able to recover between 1924 and 1928?

- Economic developments
- International agreements   (12 marks)

Part 2 Germany and the Depression, 1929–34

🚦 Knowledge test: How much do you know about Germany and the Depression, 1929–34?

Don't worry if you cannot answer all the questions in this knowledge test or if you make mistakes. You can use the core content pages to check your answers and fill in the gaps in your knowledge.

> **Revision Tip**
>
> When you have finished all the **Recall challenges**, use the page references in blue to check your answers. If you have made a mistake, **use a different colour pen to write in the correct answer**.

Recall challenges

1: Do you know the key terms?

Task: Match each key term with its correct definition or description.

Key term	Definition
Communists	A system where the government is chosen by the people (e.g. in the Weimar Republic, all adults had the right to vote for the government they wanted)
Dictatorship	A government in which multiple political parties have to co-operate to rule the country
SA	The main left-wing political party in Germany. It was supported by the working class and was the most popular party in the elections that took place in 1928 and 1930.
Social Democratic Party	When a society is ruled by one all-powerful person and there is no democracy
Coalition governments	People who believe in a society where all resources are shared out equally and there is no private property (e.g. like Russia after the revolution in 1917)
German National Party	The German word for leader; Hitler's title after the death of President Hindenburg in 1934
Trade unions	The brown-shirted gangs set up by Hitler to protect his meetings and break up the meetings of his political opponents
Centre Party	A German political party that did not support democracy and wanted Germany to return to what it was like before the Weimar Republic, when it was ruled by a monarch
Führer	Part of the Weimar Constitution which meant that the President could pass laws without going through the Reichstag
Propaganda	A German political party that wanted to protect the interests of Catholics
Emergency powers	Groups who wanted to overthrow democracy (e.g. the Nazis and the Communists during the time of the Weimar Republic)
Extremist parties	Any means of spreading political ideas in order to gain support for a political party or leader

2: Do you know the key individuals?

Task: Match each key individual with the correct description.

Key individual	Description
Paul von Hindenburg	The leader of the German Centre Party who served as German Chancellor from 1930 to 1932
Ernst Röhm	The individual in charge of Nazi propaganda
Franz von Papen	A Dutch communist who confessed to starting the Reichstag Fire
Heinrich Brüning	The leader of the SA, murdered during the Night of the Long Knives in 1934
Josef Goebbels	The leader of the German army in the First World War and President of Germany from 1925 until his death in 1934
Marinus van der Lubbe	The leader of the German Centre Party (1932–33) who agreed to form a government with Hitler

3: Do you know the key events and developments?

Task
- Answer as many of the questions below as you can.
- Mark your work using the page numbers provided. A total of 40 marks are available.
- Use the quiz to identify areas you need to revise in detail.

List three economic problems caused by the Depression in Germany.	List two political parties that saw their popularity increase as a result of the Depression.	List three promises made by the Nazis in their election campaigns between 1930 and 1932.	See pages 22–23 for the answers	Mark out of 15
List two key features of Nazi propaganda.	List three reasons why the SA was important to Hitler and the Nazi Party.	List two reasons why Hitler appealed to German people.		
List two reasons why Germany was difficult to govern between 1928 and 1932.	List two reasons why opposition to the Nazis was weak between 1928 and 1932.	List two reasons why Hindenburg replaced Brüning with Papen as Chancellor in 1932.	See pages 26–27 for the answers	Mark out of 10
Why did Papen struggle to govern Germany?	Why did Papen make a secret deal with Hitler?	List two reasons why Hindenburg agreed to Papen's plan to make Hitler Chancellor.		
List two consequences of the Reichstag Fire.	List two reasons why the Nazis were able to push through the Enabling Act.	List three ways in which Hitler was able to eliminate opposition.	See pages 28–29 for the answers	Mark out of 15
List three causes of the Night of the Long Knives.	List three consequences of the Night of the Long Knives.	What two positions did Hitler combine when he became Führer?		

Core content 2.1: The impact of the Depression and the growth in support for the Nazi Party

Exam specification checklist for this topic

- The impact of the Depression
- The growth in support for the Nazis and other extremist parties (1928–32)
- The role of the SA
- Hitler's appeal

Revision task

Use the flashcards on pages 22–23 to improve your knowledge and understanding of these topics. Test yourself by trying to answer the key questions with the bullet point answers covered up. Make a note of the topics you struggle to remember – you can spend more time on them later in your revision programme.

Key question 1: Why was the Wall Street Crash an important turning point?	• When the US stock market crashed in 1929, banks and businesses in the USA lost large sums of money. One in four people in the USA became unemployed. • The economic problems faced by the USA created serious problems for countries in Europe who traded with or borrowed money from the USA. • Germany was particularly badly hit as its economy depended on loans from America. By January 1932, one third of German workers were unemployed.
Key question 2: What economic, social and political problems were caused by the Depression? The impact of the Depression – what was **PUSHED** up? **P**overty ↑ **U**nemployment ↑ **S**upport for extreme political parties ↑ **H**omelessness, crime and violence ↑ **E**conomic problems ↑ **D**issatisfaction with the Weimar Republic ↑	**Economic problems** • Many German businesses depended on loans from the USA. They went bankrupt when the loans stopped. • German companies found that they could not sell the goods they were making. As unemployment increased, demand for goods fell. Some 50,000 businesses went bankrupt between 1929 and 1932. • Farmers struggled to sell their goods as people could not afford high food prices. By 1932, 18,000 farmers had gone bankrupt. • **Unemployment** increased to over 6 million. **Social problems** • **Poverty** increased as people lost their jobs and were forced to sell their possessions to make money. The German government could not afford to support the large numbers of people who were unemployed. Unemployment benefits were cut by 60 per cent. • **Homelessness** and crime increased. People lived in squats in disused office buildings and were forced to beg for food. • Street violence increased as young people joined street gangs. Supporters of different political parties fought each other on the streets and tried to disrupt each other's meetings. Germany seemed to be falling into chaos. **Political problems** • Many people had been optimistic and positive about the Weimar Republic during the economic recovery of the Golden Twenties. As the Depression hit, the mood of the country turned to anger and despair. • Many people in Germany, rich and poor, blamed the leaders of the Weimar Republic for the Depression. Support for the pro-democracy political parties that had run the country (the Social Democrats, the German Democratic Party, the People's Party and the Centre Party) fell. • Support for **extremist political parties**, such as the Nazis and the Communists, increased. In 1928, under 3 per cent of Germans voted for the Nazis. By the summer of 1932, this had increased to 37 per cent.

Key question 3: Why did Hitler and the Nazi Party appeal to the German people?	<ul><li>**Hitler's leadership skills and charisma** – Hitler was able to make people believe that he alone could save them from the problems facing Germany. He came across as a messiah or saviour, someone who would 'make Germany great again'. Hitler was a powerful and inspiring public speaker – he seemed to be able to connect with his audience and to fill them with a sense of hope. Hitler argued that democracy had failed Germany and that the time had come for a strong leader who would make the key decisions.</li><li>**Nazi Party policies and promises** – Some Germans liked the Nazis' foreign policy aims. In *Mein Kampf*, Hitler had promised to ignore the Treaty of Versailles, rebuild the army and unite all German-speaking people in one country. The Nazis also promised to help farmers by increasing the prices for the crops they produced.</li><li>**Fear of Communism** – As support for the Communists increased, many people began to fear that they could take over the country. German business owners and farmers feared the Communists because in the Soviet Union (after the Russian revolution), the government had taken over big industries and seized control of farmers' land. Many people voted for the Nazis as they believed that the Nazis were the only party that could stop the Communists.</li><li>**Support from rich business owners** – The Nazis raised money to pay for their election campaigns by developing links with rich business owners like Fritz Thyssen.</li></ul>
Key question 4: What were the key features of Nazi propaganda? 	Nazi propaganda was organised by Josef Goebbels.<ul><li>He used the latest technology – loudspeakers, films and cleverly designed posters – to spread the Nazi message. Hitler was frequently presented as a saviour who could solve Germany's problems and provide hope for the future. This can be seen in the 1932 Nazi election poster opposite. The slogan says 'Our last hope: Hitler'.</li><li>He organised huge rallies (some of which were attended by 100,000 people). Hitler often made a dramatic entrance, surrounded by a sea of swastikas and flags. Hitler often travelled by aeroplane so he could attend as many meetings as possible.</li></ul>
Key question 5: What role did the SA play in the rise of the Nazis?	The SA was like the Nazis' own private army. They were sometimes known as Brownshirts because of the colour of their uniforms. More than half of the SA came from the unemployed and many had been soldiers in the First World War. They played an important role in the Nazi Party:<ul><li>They protected Nazi speakers and stopped meetings being disrupted by opponents.</li><li>They helped to deliver propaganda leaflets to people's homes.</li><li>They disrupted the meetings of political opponents, especially the Communists.</li><li>With their uniform and marches, they looked disciplined and capable of bringing law and order to Germany. This attracted some voters. However, other Germans were put off by their violence and the street fights that took place with Communists.</li></ul>

Apply: Exam practice ▶

Questions 1, 2 and 3: How to approach the interpretations questions

Task
Use the advice on these pages to answer the interpretations questions below.

1. How does Interpretation B differ from Interpretation A about why the Nazi Party appealed to the people of Germany? Explain your answer using Interpretations A and B. **(4 marks)**

2. Why might the authors of Interpretations A and B have a different interpretation about why the Nazi Party appealed to the people of Germany? Explain your answer using Interpretations A and B and your contextual knowledge. **(4 marks)**

3. Which interpretation do you find most convincing about why the Nazi Party appealed to the people of Germany? Explain your answer using interpretations 1 and 2 and your contextual knowledge. **(8 marks)**

> **Exam Tips: Questions 1 and 2**
>
> For Q1: Focus on content. Identify the main message of each interpretation and the information used to support it.
>
> For Q2: Focus on the provenance. Who produced each interpretation? How might their background affect their interpretation?

INTERPRETATION A: Amy Buller, writing in her book *Darkness over Germany* (published in 1943). Buller taught in an English university but visited Germany regularly in the 1920s and 1930s. She did not support the Nazi Party, but she tried to understand why some people were attracted to the party.

As Hitler spoke I was most interested to hear the reactions of the men around me. 'He speaks for me, he speaks for me.' 'Oh God, he knows how I feel.' Many of them seemed lost to the world around them and were probably unaware of what they were saying. One man in particular struck me as he lent forward with his head in his hands, and with a sort of sob said, 'God be thanked, he understands.'

INTERPRETATION B: Albert Speer, writing in his book *Inside the Third Reich* (published in 1970). Speer joined the Nazi Party in 1931 and became Hitler's personal architect and later Nazi Minister for Weapons during the Second World War. He was sentenced to 20 years in prison after the war. In this extract, he explains why his mother joined the Nazi Party. She was married to an architect and the family suffered financially from the impact of hyperinflation.

It must have been during these months that my mother saw an SA parade in the streets. The sight of discipline in a time of chaos, the impression of energy in a time of hopelessness, seems to have won her over also. Without ever having heard a speech or read a pamphlet, she joined the party.

Question 3: How to approach the main interpretations question

The key to doing well on this question is to **use your contextual knowledge**. Start your answer by explaining why both interpretations help us understand why the Nazis grew in popularity in the period 1929–32.

Interpretation A suggests that Hitler's speeches and charisma were important reasons why the Nazis appealed to people in Germany in the early 1930s. What contextual knowledge could you bring in to support this? Explain how:
- Hitler was an important figure in Nazi election campaigns – he was flown to meetings so he could attend as many rallies as possible
- Many Germans, especially those who had suffered during the Depression, saw Hitler as a saviour and were attracted to the messages he gave in his speeches.

Interpretation B suggests that the SA played an important role in attracting support for the Nazi Party. What contextual knowledge could you bring in to support this? Explain how:
- Some Germans were impressed by the SA's organisation and discipline – how they looked capable of bringing order to Germany.
- Many Germans (like Speer's mother) had lost faith in the political parties that had run the Weimar Republic. They had lived through hyperinflation and then seen the chaos and misery caused by the Depression. To these people, the Nazis were different and seemed to offer the energy and policies that were needed to solve Germany's problems.

In your conclusion, you should make a judgement. Which interpretation is more convincing? For example, you could argue that Hitler's charisma and speeches were crucial and appealed to many Germans, whereas the SA did put off some voters due to its involvement in street violence and the way it intimidated and threatened opponents.

Question 6: How to approach the evaluate question

The interpretations questions that you have just practised explore the reasons for the growing popularity of the Nazi Party in the late 1920s and early 1930s. This topic could be the focus of an evaluation-style question at the end of your exam.

Task

Use the model explanations below to help you answer this exam question.

Which of the following was the most important reason why the Nazi Party grew in popularity between 1928 and 1932?
- **The impact of the Depression**
- **The propaganda of the Nazi Party and the charisma of Hitler**

Explain your answer with reference to both reasons. **(12 marks)**

	Key features of the explanations
Explanation 1 Nazi propaganda was very effective and played an **important role** in gaining support for the party. Unlike the Communists and other extreme groups, the Nazis were able to appeal to a wide range of different groups of people. However, the growing popularity of the Nazi Party was **mainly down to** Hitler's strong leadership and charismatic personality. **Crucially, he was able to connect with voters** and convince them that he could solve Germany's problems. Without Hitler, the Nazi Party may have struggled to make an impact.	• Comparisons are made to other groups who were less successful. • There is a clear final judgement. • This is supported by counterfactual reasoning (e.g. 'without x it is unlikely y would have happened').
Explanation 2 The Nazis were well organised, and they did have very effective propaganda, but this only partly explains why the Nazi Party grew in popularity. In 1928, the Nazis only gained 2.6 per cent of the vote and they may well have remained a small and relatively insignificant party had it not been for the Depression. This was an essential turning point. As a result of the severe economic and social problems they experienced during the Depression, German people lost faith with the Weimar Republic and Nazi policies started to appeal to voters.	• The explanation recognises that a range of factors played a role in the rise of the Nazis. • A clear judgement is made and is supported by very precise evidence. • Phrases like 'an essential turning point' help to make it clear which factors are being prioritised.

Core content 2.2: The failure of Weimar democracy

Exam specification checklist for this topic

- Election results 1928–32
- The weakening of opposition to the Nazis (1928–32)
- The role of Papen and Hindenburg in Hitler's appointment as Chancellor

Revision task

Use the flashcards on pages 26–27 to improve your knowledge and understanding of these topics. Test yourself by trying to answer the key questions with the bullet point answers covered up. Make a note of the topics you struggle to remember – you can spend more time on them later in your revision programme.

Key question 1: Why was Germany difficult to govern between 1928 and 1932?

- Weimar democracy and election results produced **coalition governments**. No political party gained more than 50 per cent of the votes in the Reichstag so parties had to join together to form coalition government.
- Each chancellor struggled to get the rest of the coalition to support their policies. For example, in 1930, **Chancellor Brüning** (the leader of the Centre Party) wanted to tackle the economic problems by cutting benefits to the unemployed. The Social Democrats, the political party with most members of the Reichstag, did not support this and refused to support his government.
- In September 1930, President Hindenburg decided to hold a new election. The **Nazis became the second largest party** in the Reichstag, making it even harder for Brüning to govern effectively.

Key question 2: Why was opposition to the Nazis weak between 1928 and 1932?

- **The opposition was divided** and refused to work together. The Nazis' two main rivals, the Communists and the Social Democrats, were bitter enemies. The Social Democrats were worried about losing votes to the Communists. Meanwhile, the Communists had developed close links with the USSR. Stalin, the leader of the USSR, did not want the German Communists to work with the Social Democrats.
- **Opposition parties underestimated the Nazis.** The Social Democrats did not think that people would fall for Nazi propaganda and they were shocked when the Nazis became the second largest party in 1930. The main political parties did not realise how angry people were with the leaders of the Weimar Republic and how prepared they were to vote for extremist parties.

Key question 3: How did Hitler become Chancellor?

Anger at Weimar Republic
Bankrupt businesses
Coalition governments
Deal with Papen
Economic problems
Fear of Communism
Goebbels' propaganda
Hitler's charisma

Key question 4: How did political events in 1932 help Hitler become Chancellor?

Step 1: Brüning loses power

- Brüning struggled to improve the economy and had to rely on President Hindenburg to use his emergency powers to pass laws without going through the Reichstag.
- Brüning angered President Hindenburg when he tried to introduce laws that would give land belonging to bankrupt landowners to poor people in the countryside.
- Hindenburg replaced Brüning with Franz von Papen (also from the Centre Party) and called a new election.

Step 2: Papen loses power

- In the elections in July 1932, the Nazis won 37 per cent of the vote and became the largest party in the Reichstag. Hitler expected to be made Chancellor but President Hindenburg appointed Papen instead.
- Papen did not have the support of any of the main political parties. The Nazis, the Communists and the Social Democrats did not support his policies. Like Brüning, Papen struggled to govern effectively.
- In November 1932, another election was held. The Nazis remained the largest party in the Reichstag, with 33 per cent of the vote.
- General von Schleicher, one of Hindenburg's main advisers, became Chancellor.

Step 3: Schleicher loses power

- Papen was angry that Schleicher had replaced him. He plotted behind Schleicher's back. As Schleicher struggled to gain support for his ideas, Papen held secret meetings with Hitler, business owners and army leaders. Papen and Hitler made a political deal – Hitler would become Chancellor and Papen Vice Chancellor.
- Papen wanted to regain power and he thought that he would be able to control Hitler. Support for the Nazis appeared to be dropping and Papen underestimated Hitler; he even boasted to a friend that 'in two months we will have pushed Hitler into a corner so that he squeaks'.
- Papen persuaded Hindenburg to remove Schleicher and replace him with Hitler as Chancellor.

Key question 5: Why did President Hindenburg agree to make Hitler Chancellor?

- Papen persuaded Hindenburg that Hitler could be controlled. Under Papen's plan only three Nazis (including Hitler) would join the 12-man cabinet that would run the country.
- Papen's plan had the support of the German elite (the army, the wealthy business owners and large landowners). They were worried about the threat of Communism and thought that Hitler could protect them from losing land, wealth and power.
- President Hindenburg was also worried about the threat of Communism and as Hitler was leader of Germany's largest political party, he reluctantly accepted Papen's plan.

Core content 2.3: The establishment of Hitler's dictatorship

Exam specification checklist for this topic

- The Reichstag Fire
- The Enabling Act
- The elimination of political opposition and the trade unions
- Röhm and the Night of the Long Knives
- Hitler becomes Führer

Revision task

Use the flashcards on pages 28–29 to improve your knowledge and understanding of these topics. Test yourself by trying to answer the key questions with the bullet point answers covered up. Make a note of the topics you struggle to remember – you can spend more time on them later in your revision programme.

Key question 1: How did the Reichstag fire help Hitler increase support and remove opposition?

On 27 February 1933, the Reichstag building in Berlin was destroyed by fire. A Dutch Communist (Marinus van der Lubbe) was found at the scene. The Nazis exploited the fire.

- Goebbels spread propaganda that Germany was under attack from the Communists. Some 4000 Communist leaders were arrested.
- Hitler persuaded President Hindenburg to use his emergency powers and introduce the Reichstag Fire Decree for the protection of the people. This decree ended the freedom of the press and the right of free speech. It meant that the Nazi government could arrest people without charge. Thousands of potential opponents of the Nazis were arrested; many were brutally tortured.
- The Nazis took control of the media and used radio to broadcast their anti-Communist message. As a result of this and funding from rich business owners (many of whom were scared of a Communist takeover), the Nazis increased their share of the vote to 44 per cent in the March elections.

Key question 2: How did Hitler push through the Enabling Act?

Hitler wanted an Enabling Act that would give him the power to pass laws for the next four years without going through the Reichstag. In order to achieve this, Hitler needed to get two-thirds of the Reichstag to support it. The Nazis only made up 44 per cent of the Reichstag but Hitler got the Enabling Act through because:

- The National Party agreed to support the Act.
- The Centre Party was persuaded to vote in favour of the Act when Hitler promised to protect the Catholic Church.
- Members of the Communist Party were banned from voting.
- Some Social Democrats stayed away from voting because they feared being attacked by the Nazi SA.

Key question 3: How did Hitler eliminate political opposition and the trade unions?

- In May 1933, trade union offices were taken over and union leaders arrested. All trade unions were merged into one organisation, the new German Labour Front (DAF). This was totally controlled by the Nazis.
- The Nazis banned the Social Democratic Party and the Communist Party. After a lot of pressure, threats and intimidation from the Nazis, the National Party and the Centre Party broke up.
- In July 1933, the Nazis passed a law banning people from forming new political parties. Germany was a one-party state, led by a leader who could pass laws without needing the support of the Reichstag.

Key question 4: What were the causes and consequences of the Night of the Long Knives?	During the night of 29 June 1934, the leading members of the SA were arrested by members of the SS (Hitler's personal bodyguard). Many were executed in what became known as the Night of the Long Knives. The leader of the SA, Ernst Röhm, was accused of plotting to overthrow Hitler. When he refused to take his own life, he was shot.	
	What were the causes of the Night of the Long Knives?	**What were the consequences of the Night of the Long Knives?**
	1 **Röhm seemed to be a threat to Hitler:** • He had criticised Hitler in a newspaper article. He did not feel that the SA had been rewarded enough since the Nazis had taken power. • Most of the SA were working-class men who wanted Hitler to introduce reforms to help the workers. Hitler was worried that if he did this, he would lose the support of the German elite (the rich business owners and landowners whose support he needed). • The SA had over 3 million members and Röhm had begun to arm them with weapons from abroad. 2 **Hitler needed the support of the army:** • Army officers did not like the SA. They viewed the SA as undisciplined thugs. • They feared that Röhm wanted to take over the army. 3 **Rivalry in the Nazi Party:** • Two leading Nazis, Goering and Himmler, did not want Röhm to have so much power. They both reported to Hitler that the SA was planning an uprising. • Himmler was the leader of the highly disciplined SS. He wanted to break away from the SA and build up the power of the SS.	1 **Hitler became more powerful and more popular:** • President Hindenburg thanked Hitler for his actions and most Germans seemed to accept what he had done (the SA was unpopular and intimidated people). • However, the Night of the Long Knives also sent a warning to the rest of Germany about how ruthless Hitler could be. • Papen was arrested and then forced to resign as Vice Chancellor. 2 **Hitler gained the support of the army:** • Hitler agreed to respect the rights of the army. In return, the army agreed to support Hitler and stay out of politics. 3 **The SS gained power and the SA lost power:** • The SS became more powerful. It was no longer under the control of the SA. • The SA became less powerful. Many members joined the SS or the army.

Key question 5: How strong was Hitler's position by the end of 1934?	• On 2 August 1934, President Hindenburg died. Hitler announced that he was combining the positions of President and Chancellor. **Hitler would now take the title of Führer**. He organised a referendum in which 90 per cent of voters said that they approved of Hitler taking up this new position. • After Hindenburg's death, **Hitler became Commander-in-Chief of the armed forces**. The army took an oath of personal loyalty to Hitler. • As a result of the Enabling Act, **Hitler could pass any law that he wanted**; he did not have to have the support of the Reichstag. • **The Nazis controlled the only trade union** – the new German Labour Front (DAF). • **The Nazi Party was the only political party** and people were banned from setting up new political parties.

Apply: Exam practice

Question 6: How to organise and communicate your ideas

> **Exam Tip**
>
> Add specific details to support your answer and prove the points you are making.
>
> We have completed a detailed plan for how you could approach this question. However, one of the ways you can improve your work is to add in specific supporting details.

Task

Add statistics and specific examples in the spaces in the plan below, and then answer the exam question below the tables.

Paragraph 1 focus: How the economic problems of the Weimar Republic contributed to Hitler becoming Chancellor

Identify the problem	Briefly **explain** why it happened	**Describe** what happened as a result of the problem	**Explain the impact and link it to the question** – How did it lead to Hitler becoming Chancellor?
The Depression	• Caused by the Wall Street Crash • Loans and investment from USA stops	• German firms and farmers went bankrupt *How many businesses?* ……………………….. *How many farms?* …….. • High unemployment (*How much?* …………..), poverty and crime • Anger at the Weimar government	• People started to turn away from the main democratic parties – support increased for extremist groups, such as the Nazis *Prove it with statistics* % of vote in 1928 = ……..% % of vote in 1932 = …….% • The Nazis used the economic problems in their propaganda posters, leaflets and speeches. For example, …………………………..

Paragraph 2 focus: How the political problems of the Weimar Republic contributed to Hitler becoming Chancellor

Identify the problem	Briefly **explain** why it happened	**Describe** what happened as a result of the problem	**Explain the impact and link it to the question** – How did it lead to Hitler becoming Chancellor?
Coalition governments	• Caused by the Weimar political system • No party got more than 50% of the vote	• Different parties disagreed • Chancellors struggled to get the support they needed to pass laws. For example, ………………… • The President had to use his emergency powers to pass laws	• People started to question whether Weimar democracy was working • They started to look for a strong leader who could solve Germany's problems • The chaos led to political deals; for example, …………………………..
Weak opposition to the Nazis	• Caused by disagreements between the Communists and the Social Democrats	• The Social Democrats felt threated by the Communist party • Stalin did not want German communists working with the Social Democrats	• The Social Democrats and the Communists did not work together to stop the Nazis • The policies of the Communists scared many voters, especially the ………………… and ………………, many of whom voted Nazi to stop the Communists getting into power

Which of the following was the most important reason why Hitler was appointed Chancellor in January 1933?

- The economic problems of the Weimar Republic
- The political problems of the Weimar Republic

(12 marks)

Apply: Further exam practice

Which of the following was the most important reason why Hitler was able to establish a dictatorship?

- Germany's economic and political problems
- The actions taken by Hitler and the Nazi Party **(12 marks)**

> *Paragraph 1 — Germany's economic and political problems helped Hitler establish a dictatorship*
> - *The impact of the Depression*
> - *The Reichstag fire*
>
> *Paragraph 2 — The actions taken by Hitler and the Nazi Party helped them establish a dictatorship*
> - *Asking Hindenburg to agree to the Reichstag Fire Decree*
> - *Pushing through the Enabling Act*
> - *Eliminating opposition — the trade unions and political parties*

Exam Tip: Organise your ideas

You will notice that we use a planning grid, like the one on page 30, to show you how to organise your ideas. In the exam, you will not have time to plan in as much detail as this but you should still make a quick plan. The example below shows you what a quick plan should look like.

- Aim to decide on the focus or main argument of the paragraph.
- Then jot down content you can include to support this argument.

Task

1. Use the plan above to write the first two paragraphs of an answer to the exam question. Remember that when you write your answer, you should work through the process we have modelled in our detailed planning grids.

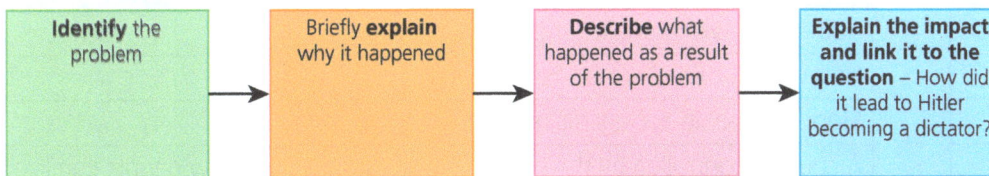

Identify the problem → Briefly explain why it happened → Describe what happened as a result of the problem → Explain the impact and link it to the question – How did it lead to Hitler becoming a dictator?

2. Use the exam tips below to write your conclusion. Aim to demonstrate complex thinking by:
   - **Explaining links between the reasons** why Hitler was able to establish a dictatorship. What is the relationship between the causes? Did economic and political problems create opportunities that Hitler and the Nazis then exploited? Without the Reichstag fire, it may have been difficult for Hitler to push through the Enabling Act.
   - **Thinking carefully about the language you use to describe the key events and developments.** Match the factors in the table on the right with the right language to show what role the factor played in establishing a dictatorship.

Factor that helped Hitler	The role it played
The Depression	A **crucial turning point**, this **transformed** the German political system, **ending** Weimar democracy and **creating** a situation where Hitler did not have to go through the Reichstag to pass laws.
The Reichstag fire	A longer-term cause that **laid the platform** for Hitler, **creating a climate** in which people lost faith in Weimar democracy and were more willing to accept strong leadership.
The Enabling Act	The **final blow** to Weimar democracy, it **removed** any chance of opposition forming against the Nazis and meant that Germany was now a one-party state.
The ban on new political parties being formed	An **important trigger cause**, that **provided an opportunity** for Hitler to attack the Communist Party and intimidate opponents.

Part 3 The experiences of Germans under the Nazis, 1933–45

🚦 Knowledge test: How much do you know about the experiences of Germans under the Nazis, 1933–45?

Don't worry if you cannot answer all the questions in this knowledge test or if you make mistakes. You can use the core content pages to check your answers and fill in the gaps in your knowledge.

> **Revision Tip**
>
> When you have finished all the **Recall challenges**, use the page references in blue to check your answers. If you have made a mistake, **use a different colour pen to write in the correct answer**.

Recall challenges

1: Do you know the key terms?

Task
Match each key term with its correct definition or description.

Key term	Definition
Public works programmes	Hatred of Jewish people
Rearmament	Nazi word for the German 'race'
Self-sufficiency	Stopping people accessing information and ideas
Rationing	A country controlled by the police with strict rules over how people can live
Conscription	Employment schemes financed by the government to provide jobs
Aryan	Forcing people to do military service
Antisemitism	Spreading political ideas and gaining support for your political party
Propaganda	The Nazi programme to rebuild the strength of the army
Censorship	Creating an economy which produces everything that a country needs
Police state	The government-controlled sharing out of food, fuel and clothes

2: Do you know the key individuals?

Task
Match each key individual with the correct description.

Key individual	Description
Joseph Goebbels	In charge of the four year plan to ready the German economy for war
Hermann Goering	A Catholic bishop who criticised the Nazi euthanasia policy
Heinrich Himmler	In charge of the SS, the police and the Gestapo
Bishop von Galen	This person was in charge of Nazi propaganda
Martin Niemöller	Army officer who organised the July 1944 Bomb Plot against Hitler
Claus von Stauffenberg	The person who set up the non-Nazi Confessional Church

3: Do you know the key events and developments?

Task
- Answer as many of the questions below as you can.
- Mark your work using the page numbers provided. A total of 60 marks are available.
- Use the quiz to identify areas you need to revise in detail.

List three reasons why the Nazis were able to reduce unemployment.	List two ways in which economic policies prepared Germany for war.	List two groups of people who benefitted from Nazi economic policies.	See pages 34–35 for the answers	Mark out of 15
List three negative impacts of Nazi economic policies for workers.	List two ways in which the DAF (German Labour Front) tried to improve working conditions.	List three ways in which the Second World War affected the lives of people in Germany.		
List three aims of Nazi social policies towards women.	List three ways in which the lives of women changed as a result of Nazi social policies.	What was the Nazi slogan that made it clear what they wanted women to focus on?	See pages 36–37 for the answers	Mark out of 15
List two aims of the Hitler Youth.	List three examples of activities that young people would do in the Hitler Youth.	List three ways in which education and the school curriculum changed?		
What was the name given to Hitler's agreement with the Catholic Church?	What was the name of the Protestant Church under the control of the Nazis?	What was the name of the Protestant Church set up in opposition to the Nazis?	See pages 38–39 for the answers	Mark out of 10
List three groups that were persecuted by Nazi social policy and practice.	List three ways in which Jewish people were persecuted between 1933 and 1938.	What was the name of the conference at which the Final Solution was planned?		
List two examples of how Goebbels censored culture in Nazi Germany.	List two examples of how Goebbels used culture as propaganda in Nazi Germany.	List two ways in which Nazi culture was different from Weimar culture.	See pages 40–41 for the answers	Mark out of 10
List two roles played by the SS in the Nazi police state created by Himmler.	What was the name given to the secret police?	How many offences were punishable by the death penalty by 1943?		
List two examples of opposition to the Nazis from youth groups.	List two ways in which the White Rose protested against Nazi rule.	Give one reason why some army generals turned against Hitler.	See pages 42–43 for the answers	Mark out of 10
Give one example of opposition from the army.	List two examples of opposition from the Church.	List two reasons why the Nazis faced so little opposition.		

Core content 3.1: Economic changes

> **Exam specification checklist for this topic**
> - How the Nazis reduced unemployment – public works schemes
> - Benefits and drawbacks for workers
> - Preparing Germany for war – rearmament and self-sufficiency
> - The impact of war on the economy and the German people

> **Revision task**
> Use the flashcards on pages 34–35 to improve your knowledge and understanding of these topics. Test yourself by trying to answer the key questions with the bullet point answers covered up. Make a note of the topics you struggle to remember – you can spend more time on them later in your revision programme.

Key question 1: How did Nazi economic policies reduce unemployment?

The 4 Rs

Roads and railways

Through **public works programmes**, 2000 miles of new motorways (**autobahns**) were built.
- Railways were extended and new canals and bridges were built to improve transport.
- These public works programmes provided jobs for unemployed workers.

RAD

In 1935, it became compulsory for all 19–25-year-old men to do six months' labour service in the **RAD (National Labour Service)**.
- In the RAD, the work was hard and the rules were strict. The young men were paid very little money and often had to live away from home.

Rearmament

The Nazi government invested a lot of money in building new tanks, aeroplanes and battleships. This created millions of jobs in the factories.
- It also meant that the iron, steel and chemicals industries grew and needed more workers.
- In 1935, **conscription** was introduced. All males aged 18–25 had to do two years' military service. This increased the armed forces from 100,000 to 1.4 million and greatly reduced unemployment.

Registers

Lots of people were taken off the **unemployment register** – for example, young people working in the RAD were not counted.
- Women were pressured into giving up paid work.
- Many Jewish people lost their jobs and were not included on the unemployment registers.

Key question 2: How did Nazi economic policies prepare Germany for war?

In 1936, Hitler placed Hermann Goering in charge of a **four-year plan** to make Germany ready for war. Goering soon started to argue with **Hjalmar Schacht**, the Nazis' economic minister. Schacht's policies (public works programmes) had helped to reduce unemployment and he now wanted to focus on producing consumer goods rather than armaments. Schacht resigned in 1937, leaving Goering to make all the important economic decisions.

Goering had two main aims:
- **Rearmament** – From 1936, two-thirds of government spending went on rearmament. Millions of Germans worked in factories producing military equipment, uniforms and weapons.
- **Self-sufficiency** – To make sure that Germany could produce all the goods it needed so that it did not have to rely on imports from other countries.

Key question 3: What were the benefits and drawbacks of Nazi economic policies?

Social group	Benefits	Drawbacks
Business owners	• Some factory owners benefitted from rearmament. • The Nazis destroyed trade unions, meaning that factory owners could keep wages low and increase working hours without facing strikes.	• The focus on rearmament meant that firms producing consumer goods lost out. • Small businesses went bankrupt as they struggled to compete with the larger firms.
Farmers	• Farmers had their debts cancelled and food prices increased. • **Farmers'** incomes increased by 41% between 1933 and 1936.	• Later on, farmers struggled to find enough workers as people went to work in the large factories and the focus was on rearmament.
Workers	• Public works programmes provided employment. By 1939, only 35,000 men were unemployed. • The average wage in 1936 was ten times higher than unemployment pay. • The **DAF (German Labour Front)** introduced a scheme called the **Beauty of Labour** to improve working conditions and provide low-cost food and shower rooms in the workplace. • The DAF created **Strength through Joy** to improve leisure opportunities. It organised sports programmes, art exhibitions, cheap hiking trips and holidays.	• Workers had no rights. Trade unions were abolished, and the Nazis set up the German Labour Front (DAF). People struggled to get work if they were not a member. • Workers could not go on strike if their pay was cut or if they had to work longer hours. The DAF did what employers asked and did not stand up for workers. • Most workers worked longer hours. • Those working in agriculture or producing consumer goods saw their wages decrease. • During the war, there were labour shortages. Holidays were banned and working hours were increased to a minimum of 60 hours per week.
Young men in the RAD	• Those who had been unemployed now had a job and were given food and lodging (in barracks).	• The men were paid very little money, often had to live away from home and were treated like they were in the army.

Key question 4: In what ways did the lives of the German people change during the Second World War?

Reduction in workers

Return of women to the workplace

Rationing

a) **Economic problems**
- By 1944, 13 million men were serving in the German army. This created labour shortages. Workers were forced to work extra shifts.
- There were shortages of oil, steel and fuel.
- The Nazis tried to solve labour shortages by encouraging women to return to the workplace.
- Food shortages were caused by large numbers of farm workers joining the army.
- Rationing restricted Germans to a diet of bread, potatoes and vegetables. Fish, eggs, milk and cheese were hard to come by.

Rubble

Refugees

b) **Social problems**
- British and American bombing raids reduced many homes to rubble. Two million homes were destroyed, along with factories, roads and railways.
- In the east of Germany many people became refugees as they fled from the Russian army that was advancing into Germany. Cold, hunger and disease meant that over half a million Germans died fleeing west.

All led to …
Resentment

c) **Political problems**
- In the early stages of the war, the German people's morale was high because the war was going well. However, from 1943, morale and support for the war started to drop; anger and resentment against the Nazi Party increased.

Core content 3.2: Nazi social policy and practice – the impact on women and young people

Exam specification checklist for this topic

- The reasons for Nazi social policies towards women and young people
- The impact of Nazi social policies on women
- The impact of Nazi social policies on young people
- Changes in education

Revision task

Use the flashcards on pages 36–37 to improve your knowledge and understanding of these topics. Test yourself by trying to answer the key questions with the bullet point answers covered up. Make a note of the topics you struggle to remember – you can spend more time on them later in your revision programme.

Key question 1: What were Nazi social policies towards women and what impact did they have?

- *Kinder*, *Küche* and *Kirche* became the Nazi slogan which make it clear what the Nazis wanted women to focus on. It translates as **Children, Cooking and Church**.

Aims	Examples	Impact
Children The Nazis believed that German women had a duty to produce strong, racially pure children. They were worried that during the 1920s the birth rate had fallen. Nazi leaders wanted to expand and take over territory – to do this they needed a larger population.	• Abortion and the use of birth control was restricted. • Not everyone could have children. People with inherited diseases were sterilised. • Loans were offered to couples to encourage them to get married (about half a year's pay). The more children they had, the less they had to pay back (if they had four children they paid nothing back). • Medals were awarded for having children (a gold for eight children). • Divorce was made easier for people in childless marriages.	• The number of babies born increased. However, during the war, birth rates started to fall. • The number of marriages increased by a third.
Cooking The Nazis believed that men were better suited to leadership roles and fighting for the country, while women were better at bringing up children, cooking and cleaning. They believed that women should not have a political or professional role.	• All women employed by the state (e.g. doctors, teachers and civil servants) were sacked. • Employers were encouraged to employ men in favour of women. • Women were banned from the Reichstag and from becoming judges and lawyers. • The number of women allowed to go to university was restricted to 10%.	• The number of women in work went up. The Nazis were forced to employ more women because of a growing economy (during the 1930s) and labour shortages (during the war).
Church The Nazis believed that some women had the wrong type of lifestyle during the Weimar period. They wanted women to have a 'healthy lifestyle' and go to church – rather than taking an interest in fashion and going out to clubs.	• Slimming, smoking and late nights were frowned upon and exercise and going to church was encouraged. • Women were encouraged to wear simple, traditional clothes rather than fashionable clothes. • Using make-up or having permed or dyed hair was frowned upon.	• Fashionably dressed women were told off in public. • Some restaurants banned women from smoking.

Key question 2: What were the aims of the Hitler Youth and what impact did it have on young people?

LOYALTY

SOLDIERS

MOTHERS

Aims	Impact
To encourage patriotism (love of your country) and admiration for and **loyalty to Hitler**	• The Nazis shut down youth groups that they did not approve of. • By 1939, 80% of young people belonged to one of the Hitler Youth groups. • Boys and girls had to swear a personal oath, promising to love and be faithful to Hitler. • They had to answer questions on Nazi ideas and German history.
To produce fit, determined, brave and **tough male soldiers** who could fight for Germany during times of war	• Boys would join the *Pimpfen* (or 'Little Fellows') from the age of six. They wore versions of SA uniforms with swastika armbands and were taught military skills straight away. • Boys had to do combat exercise and were given physical tests (e.g. having to complete a one-and-a half-day cross-country march or to jump out of a first-floor window wearing full army battledress).
To produce young **women who could raise healthy Aryan children** and look after the home	• Girls would join the Young Girls League from the age of ten. From the ages of 14 to 18, they were members of the League of German Maidens. • The focus was on keeping fit and developing home-making skills (e.g. how to make a bed).

Key question 3: How did education change as a result of Nazi social policies?

The Nazi Teachers' League:
- Everyone had to go to school between the ages of 6 and 14.
- In order to control the education system, the Nazis made sure they controlled teachers. Teachers who refused to teach what the Nazis wanted were sacked (around 20 per cent of teachers were sacked in 1933). Nearly all teachers were members of the Nazi Teachers' League and textbooks were rewritten to fit Nazi ideas.
- Classrooms were covered in swastika flags and photos of Hitler. Pupils had to greet their teachers with the Nazi salute.

The Nazi school curriculum:
The school curriculum was changed to keep the focus on teaching young people what the Nazis wanted them to think and be able to do in the future. For example:
- The number of **PE** lessons was increased – the Nazis wanted boys to become fit and healthy soldiers. Boxing was compulsory for boys. Girls were taught home-making and childcare.
- In **history**, pupils were taught about the 'heroic' rise of the Nazis, the 'unfair' Treaty of Versailles and the 'dangers' of Communism.
- In **biology**, pupils were told about the 'superiority of the Aryan race'. They were taught that other races were 'inferior'.
- In **geography**, pupils were taught about the lands that had been taken from Germany and the need for *Lebensraum* (living space) for the German people.

Core content 3.3: Nazi social policy and practice – religion and racial persecution

Exam specification checklist for this topic
- Control of churches and religion
- Aryan ideas, racial policy and persecution
- The Final Solution

Revision task
Use the flashcards on pages 38–39 to improve your knowledge and understanding of these topics. Test yourself by trying to answer the key questions with the bullet point answers covered up. Make a note of the topics you struggle to remember – you can spend more time on them later in your revision programme.

Key question 1: How did the Nazis try to gain control over the churches?	Many Germans had strong Christian beliefs and regularly attended church. Although Hitler hated Christianity, he did not want to anger a large number of people by closing down the churches. He therefore had to move carefully. a) A concordat with the Catholic Church:<ul><li>In 1933 Hitler made an agreement with the Roman Catholic Church. A **concordat** was signed by the Pope. The Catholic Church promised that it would not interfere in politics; in return, the Nazis would not interfere with religion.</li><li>Catholic bishops had to take an oath of loyalty to the Nazi state.</li><li>Catholic priests who criticised the Nazis were sent to concentration camps.</li><li>In 1936, Catholic youth groups were forced to merge with the Hitler Youth.</li></ul>b) All Protestant churches were brought together in one official **Reich Church**:<ul><li>Bishop Ludweig Müller, the leader of the new Reich Church, declared his support for Hitler and Nazi policies.</li><li>All Reich Church services had to begin and end with the 'Heil Hitler' salute.</li><li>In 1936, all church youth groups were stopped and, by 1939, nearly all church schools had been closed down.</li><li>Reich Church pastors had to swear an oath of loyalty to Hitler. However, many refused and nearly 6000 joined a new, non-Nazi, **Confessional Church**.</li></ul>

Key question 2: How did Nazi social and racial policies lead to persecution and mass murder?

Who did the Nazis persecute?	Why were these groups persecuted?	How were they persecuted?
'Non-Aryans'<ul><li>Black people</li><li>Jewish people</li><li>Roma and Sinti people (sometimes referred to as Gypsies)</li></ul>	Hitler believed that 'true Germans' were 'Aryans' and were part of a northern European racial group that was superior to all other races. Hitler wanted the Aryan race to be kept pure. Aryans were not allowed to marry or have children with other races.	<ul><li>385 black Germans were compulsorily sterilised.</li><li>As Germany invaded Europe around 500,000 Roma and Sinti people were murdered.</li><li>During the Holocaust, six million Jewish men, women and children were murdered by the Nazis and their collaborators across Europe.</li></ul>
People with physical disabilities and mental health conditions	Hitler regarded people with disabilities and mental health conditions as a 'burden' that would 'weaken' the Aryan race.	<ul><li>350,000 people who had inherited conditions were compulsorily sterilised.</li><li>In 1939, the Nazis began a policy they called 'euthanasia', although the people they killed had no choice. By 1941, 71,000 people classed as having mental or physical disabilities had been murdered.</li></ul>
Gay people	Hitler did not approve of homosexuality and he thought it would 'weaken' Germany.	<ul><li>Around 15,000 gay men were arrested and sent to concentration camps.</li></ul>

Key question 3: In what ways were the lives of Jewish people affected by Nazi policies?

- In 1933, Jewish people made up less than 1 per cent of Germany's population but they played an important role in society. They made up 17 per cent of all bankers and 16 per cent of all lawyers.
- Hitler was obsessive in his hatred towards the Jewish people. He blamed them for the problems in Germany and Nazi propaganda portrayed them as an 'inferior' race.

The key stages in Nazi racial policy towards Jewish people	Examples of Nazi persecution	The impact on Jewish people
Step 1: Boycotts and bans (1933–34)	• The Nazis encouraged a boycott of Jewish shops. • Jewish people were banned from all state jobs (including teaching, journalism and law).	• Jewish people struggled to make enough money to survive.
Step 2: Persecution through the law (1935–38)	• In 1935, the Nazis introduced the **Nuremberg Laws**. All Jewish people lost German citizenship and could not vote. • In 1938, further laws were introduced, banning Jewish people from owning their own business, going to cinemas or attending state schools.	• Jewish people lost their rights and felt excluded from society.
Step 3: Attacks on people and property increased (1938–39)	• Goebbels introduced a campaign of violence against Jewish people. He said this was in retaliation for a Jewish student shooting a German diplomat in Paris. • Nazi Party members and the SS attacked Jewish people and destroy their homes and synagogues. The event became known as **Kristallnacht** (or 'The night of broken glass').	• 91 Jewish people were killed and 30,000 were taken to concentration camps. • Jewish people felt in danger and those who could started to emigrate.
Step 4: The impact of the Second World War and the Final Solution (1939–45)	• After Germany invaded Poland (1939), 3.5 million Jewish people found themselves trapped under Nazi rule. They were forced into **ghettos**, walled off from the rest of a town or city. Water and power supplies were cut off and food was limited. • In 1941, as the German army invaded the USSR, SS units called **Einsatzgruppen** rounded up and murdered Jewish people. • In January 1942, Nazi leaders met at the **Wannsee Conference** to plan the **'Final Solution'** to the 'Jewish question' in Europe. Europe's Jewish population would be transported to death camps where they would be murdered. At camps like Auschwitz, gas chambers capable of killing 2000 people at once were built, alongside large ovens for burning the bodies.	It is estimated that: • 500,000 Jewish people died of disease or starvation in ghettos • 1.5 million were murdered by the Einsatzgruppen • 500,000 died as a result of slave labour • 6 million Jewish people had been murdered by the end of the war.

Core content 3.4: How Hitler kept control

Exam specification checklist for this topic

- Goebbels and the use of propaganda and censorship
- Nazi culture
- Repression and the police state – the roles of Himmler, the SS and Gestapo

Revision task

Use the flashcards on pages 40–41 to improve your knowledge and understanding of these topics. Test yourself by trying to answer the key questions with the bullet point answers covered up. Make a note of the topics you struggle to remember – you can spend more time on them later in your revision programme.

Key question 1: How did Goebbels use propaganda and censorship to help the Nazis control ideas and culture?

- Goebbels used propaganda to persuade German people to support the Nazis. The key messages were that Nazi ideas were correct and that the Nazis were achieving great things.
- Goebbels used censorship to prevent the German people from hearing, seeing or reading anything that went against Nazi ideas or criticised the Nazi Party.

Feature of Nazi culture	How did Goebbels use this for propaganda?	How did Goebbels use censorship in this area?
Rallies	• At Nuremberg, rallies were attended by hundreds of thousands of people. • They were stage-managed – using searchlights, music, parades and flags to create an image of unity and power.	• Rallies to protest against the Nazi government or encourage opposition were banned.
Newspapers	• Goebbels' Ministry of Propaganda sent out daily instructions to newspapers telling them what to print. • Stories praised Hitler and contained negative stories about opponents and Jewish people.	• If they did not print what Goebbels wanted, the newspapers were closed down. • By 1939, the Nazis owned two-thirds of German newspapers.
Radio	• The availability of cheap radios meant more people could listen to Nazi propaganda. By 1939, 70% of Germans owned a radio. • Programmes focused on Hitler's speeches, German music and German history. • Loudspeakers were set up in public squares, cafés and bars so people could hear important announcements.	• People caught listening to foreign stations faced the death penalty.
Films	• Most films were adventure or love stories but a newsreel film, showing Nazi success stories, was usually played before the film.	• Goebbels controlled all the films that were made in Germany. • Scripts were checked by his ministry to check they did not contain anti-Nazi ideas.
Literature, music and art	• Goebbels encouraged books about the glory of war. • The Nazis promoted traditional German folk music and German composers such as Bach, Beethoven and Mozart. • In 1937, the Nazis opened the House of German Art. This only showed art that the Nazis approved of (such as heroic military figures or the ideal Aryan family).	• The Nazis organised book burnings (e.g. in 1933, in Berlin, students burnt 20,000 books the Nazis did not approve of). • Jazz music was banned (the Nazis saw it as music made by black people who were not part of the Aryan race). • Hitler disliked the 'modern' art produced during the Weimar period. In 1936, 5000 paintings the Nazis disapproved of were burnt.

Key question 2: How did Himmler create a police state in Nazi Germany?

- The Nazis allowed no opposition. Himmler's job was to remove any threat to Nazi rule.
- Himmler was head of a police state that spied on people, intimidated people and punished people if they stepped out of line.

Feature of the police state	What role did it play?	What was the impact on the German people?
The police and the law courts	<ul><li>The top jobs in the police were given to high-ranking Nazis.</li><li>The courts were also under Nazi control as judges were appointed by the Nazis.</li></ul>	<ul><li>The number of offences carrying the death penalty went up from 3 in 1933 to 46 in 1943.</li><li>People lived in fear – even telling an anti-Nazi joke could carry a death sentence.</li></ul>
Concentration camps	<ul><li>The Nazis set up concentration camps as soon as they came to power.</li><li>Conditions in the camps were brutal. Many people died in the camps from beatings, disease and starvation.</li></ul>	<ul><li>The threat of the camps discouraged opposition and protest.</li><li>They held anyone who criticised the Nazis (e.g. Communists, Socialists, trade unionists).</li></ul>
The SS	<ul><li>By 1939, the SS had nearly 250,000 members. It had originally been Hitler's bodyguard and members were trained to be ruthless and totally loyal to Hitler.</li><li>SS Death's Head units ran the concentration camps and death camps.</li></ul>	<ul><li>People feared the SS. It could arrest people without trial, search houses and confiscate property.</li><li>It provided an image of the Nazis being all powerful and totally in control.</li></ul>
The Gestapo	<ul><li>The Gestapo was the secret police. It spied on people, opened mail and kept detailed records on potential opponents.</li><li>It had the power to arrest people without trial and torture them for information.</li><li>In the early years, it focused on political opponents. In later years, it also targeted Jewish people and gay people.</li></ul>	<ul><li>Ordinary Germans feared the Gestapo and thought it was everywhere. It led to people feeling that they were constantly being watched and could not step out of line.</li><li>In reality, there were just 15,000 Gestapo officers to cover a population of 60 million.</li><li>This meant that the Gestapo had to depend on a network of informers who could pass on information to it.</li></ul>
Block leaders and informers	<ul><li>Every town was divided into small groups of houses, called blocks. The block leader, a local Nazi, visited every home in the block once a week.</li><li>Block leaders collected information and checked up on everyone. The block leader wrote a report on everyone in their block and noticed any signs of disobedience (e.g. not flying a Nazi flag on celebration days).</li></ul>	<ul><li>The Gestapo relied on this network of informers and block leaders for information.</li><li>It created a system where you did not know who to trust as ordinary Germans informed on work colleagues, neighbours and even family members.</li></ul>

Core content 3.5: Opposition and resistance

Exam specification checklist for this topic
- The White Rose group
- Swing Youth
- The Edelweiss Pirates
- Opposition from the Church
- The July 1944 Bomb Plot

Revision task

Use the flashcards on pages 42–43 to improve your knowledge and understanding of these topics. Test yourself by trying to answer the key questions with the bullet point answers covered up. Make a note of the topics you struggle to remember – you can spend more time on them later in your revision programme.

Key question 1: What opposition did the Nazis face from the Church?

- Remember, the Nazis had made a **concordat** (see page 38) with the Catholic Church and set up a Reich Church for all Protestants.
- A total of 6000 Protestant pastors left the Reich Church and joined the new, non-Nazi, **Confessional Church**. One of the founders, **Martin Niemöller**, was arrested and sent to a concentration camp. However, only 50 Protestant pastors (out of 17,000) and one bishop were put in prison for opposition.
- In the Catholic Church, most opposition came from individuals within the Church, rather than the Church as a whole. **Bishop von Galen** (the Catholic Bishop of Munster) criticised Nazi racist policies in his sermons. In 1941, his speeches against their euthanasia policy (the murder of people the Nazis classed as having mental or physical disabilities – see page 38) led to it being halted.

Key question 2: What opposition did the Nazis face from young people?

The White Rose:
- This was a group of students at Munich University – led by Hans Scholl, Sophie Scholl and Christoph Probst. The White Rose was disgusted at the lack of opposition to the Nazis and the persecution of Jewish people.
- The group spread anti-Nazi messages through posters, graffiti and leaflets – urging Germans to overthrow Hitler and sabotage the war effort. In 1943, it organised the first large-scale demonstration in Germany when it took to the streets and handed out anti-Nazi leaflets.
- The Nazis responded by arresting and executing the leaders of the White Rose.

The Edelweiss Pirates:
- This was an organisation of young people (mainly aged 14 to 18) who refused to behave in a way that the Nazis wanted. They sometimes wore an Edelweiss flower on their clothing. They smoked, drank alcohol and wore clothes the Nazis did not like. Some listened to foreign radio stations, others picked fights with the Hitler Youth.
- Numbers grew during the war to around 2000 but it was not a united organisation. Local groups tended to do their own thing. Some wrote anti-Nazi graffiti on walls, others distributed anti-Nazi leaflets or helped army deserters.
- In December 1942, the Gestapo arrested 739 Edelweiss Pirates in Dusseldorf. Some were put on trial and executed, others were sent to concentration camps.

Swing Youth:
- Members tended to be from wealthier backgrounds than the Edelweiss Pirates. They were less interested in politics than the White Rose and more interested in American fashion and music.
- They listened to jazz music and met in nightclubs and bars. Boys grew their hair long, while girls wore brightly coloured make-up.
- The Nazis responded by closing down the clubs and bars where Swing Youth met. Some members were arrested by the Gestapo and sent to concentration camps.

Key question 3: Why did the Nazis face some opposition from army leaders?	• Opposition to Hitler from the army mainly came from high-ranking officers. They did not like Hitler's interference with military tactics and they thought that he made rash decisions (for example, to invade the USSR in 1941). • When the war started to go badly in 1943 opposition increased and there were a number of army plots to assassinate Hitler. • The one that came closest to success was organised by **Claus von Stauffenberg** and was called the July 1944 Bomb Plot (see below). Stauffenberg had supported the Nazis in the 1930s because he thought that Hitler was the best person to stop the Communists getting into power. However, during the war, he was disgusted by Nazi policies towards Jewish people and by 1943 he had become convinced that Hitler was leading Germany to defeat.
Key question 4: Why did the July 1944 Bomb Plot fail and what were the consequences?	• Stauffenberg plotted with other high-ranking officers in the army. Their plan was to assassinate Hitler by planting a bomb at his military headquarters. They believed that Hitler's death would create an opportunity for army officers to seize power and end the war. • Stauffenberg planted a bomb at a meeting that Hitler attended. The bomb went off and four people were killed, but Hitler was only injured and survived. • After Stauffenberg had left the meeting, someone had moved the briefcase containing the bomb slightly further away from Hitler, to the other side of a heavy table leg. In addition, as it was a hot day, the windows in the room where the meeting took place were left open, meaning that the force of the blast was lessened. These chance events probably saved Hitler's life. • When Stauffenberg arrived in Berlin, he was convinced his plan had worked and Hitler was dead. However, the plot was quickly uncovered and Stauffenberg was arrested and shot. Other army leaders involved in the plot either took their own lives or were rounded up and executed. • Hitler never really recovered from the attempt on his life. He suffered physically from injuries sustained in the attack and became increasingly mentally unstable and paranoid that the army was continuing to plot behind his back.
Key question 5: Why did the Nazis face so little opposition?	The Nazis faced very little opposition. People might have moaned or complained about the Nazis in private but there was little public criticism of the Nazi government. The factors in the left-hand column of the table below played an important role.

Task

Use what you have learnt from Part 3 of this book to complete the table below. Give examples and explain why each factor was important in limiting opposition. Try to complete the table from memory, then check your answers using the page references provided.

Factor	Examples	What impact did it have?
Successful economic policies (pages 34–35)	• Reduced unemployment • Public works schemes	• Economic success boosted the popularity of the Nazis
Fear and terror (page 41)		
Propaganda and censorship (page 40)		
Control over education and youth groups (page 37)		
Control over the churches (page 38)		

Apply: Exam practice

Revisiting Questions 1, 2 and 3: How to answer the interpretations questions

1. How does Interpretation A differ from Interpretation B about how young people responded to the Hitler Youth? **(4 marks)**
2. Why might the authors of Interpretations A and B have a different view about how young people responded to the Hitler Youth? **(4 marks)**
3. Which interpretation gives the most convincing view of how young people responded to the Hitler Youth? **(8 marks)**

INTERPRETATION A: Henry Metelmann, joined the Hitler Youth in 1933. An extract from his biography, *A Hitler Youth: Growing up in Germany in the 1930s*, published in 1992.

I thought the uniform was smashing, the dark brown, the black, the swastika and all the shiny leather. Before we joined, we rarely had a decent football to play with, the Hitler Youth provided us with decent sports equipment, gymnasiums and swimming pools. Never had I been on a real holiday – my father was much too poor. Now under Hitler, for very little money I could go on lovely camps in the mountains, by the rivers or near the sea. I liked the comradeship, the marching, the sport and the war games. We were brought up to love our Führer, who was to me like a second God. When we were told about his great love for us, the German nation, I was often close to tears. I was convinced that because of my German blood that I was a superior being.

INTERPRETATION B: From the memories of A. Klonne, a young boy who became a Hitler Youth leader. Klonne published his recollections in a book, *Youth in the Third Reich*, in 1982.

I found the rules and the requirement of absolute obedience unpleasant. The Hitler Youth was interfering everywhere in people's private lives. In our troop the activities consisted almost entirely of boring military drill. The slightest faults with uniforms, the slightest lateness on parade were punished with extra drill. We were drilled in toughness and blind obedience. At the command 'down' we had to throw ourselves with bare knees onto the gravel; when we were doing press-ups, our noses were pushed in the sand; anyone who got a stitch cross-country running was made fun of as a weakling.

Exam Tips

Remember you have already practised these types of question. Look back at the advice we gave on pages 24–25 before you attempt the practice questions on this page.

Question 1

- Focus on the content of both interpretations and link this to the focus of the question (in this case, how young people responded to the Hitler Youth).
- Start your answer by identifying the main difference between each interpretation. Is the author of Interpretation A describing a positive or negative experience of the Hitler Youth? How about the author of Interpretation B?
- Then use the information in the interpretations to support your answer. What does each author refer to in their account of life in the Hitler Youth? What specific things made it a positive or negative experience for them?

Question 2

- Focus on the provenance of the interpretation. Who produced each interpretation?
- Think carefully about how the **author's background** might affect their interpretation and use your contextual knowledge. If the author came from a poor background, they might have had a different view of the Hitler Youth than someone who grew up with richer parents. Remember the impact the Depression had on Germany. For children from working-class backgrounds, the Hitler Youth offered things that they would not otherwise have experienced, such as holidays and access to good sports facilities.
- In the exam, read the provenance of the interpretation carefully. Underline details that may affect the author's point of view. For example, consider:

Their age	Their gender	Their class and wealth
Their political views	Their life experiences	The time period they are talking about

Exam Tips: Question 3

The key to doing well on this question is to use your contextual knowledge. Look at the model answer below. The key features of a strong answer have been identified for you.

Features of a high-level answer to Question 3 | Student answer

The first two paragraphs start with a clear focus on the question. They explain how both interpretations help us understand how young people responded to the Hitler Youth. There is not a 'right' and 'wrong' interpretation.

The student brings in strong contextual knowledge to support their evaluation of both interpretations. They place the events being described in their historical context.

The student has made careful word choices to show their main line of argument. By using phrases like 'some' and 'the vast majority' they make it clear which interpretation is the most convincing. In using these words, they also show an understanding that not all young people had the same experience.

The answer displays evidence of complex thinking. The student understands that responses to the Hitler Youth changed over time.

They also show an understanding that different social groups responded differently to the experience (in this case, young people from working class backgrounds tended to be more positive about their experiences).

Interpretation A helps us understand how many young people responded to the Hitler Youth. Many young people, especially those like Henry Metelmann who were from working class backgrounds, enjoyed their time in the Hitler Youth when they joined up. They would have grown up during the time of the Depression, a period of high unemployment, and life would have been tough for many families. The Hitler Youth provided young people with new experiences, like going on holiday and access to swimming pools. The Hitler Youth was a successful movement even before the Nazis came into power. Most young people joined the Hitler Youth voluntarily. It was not until 1939 that membership became compulsory.

Interpretation B helps us understand that not all young people responded positively to their time in the Hitler Youth. Klonne's account shows us that some youngsters found life in the Hitler Youth unpleasant. As time went on, the Hitler Youth became far stricter and more closely linked to preparing for war. Some young people, like Klonne, grew bored with the focus on military drills and this is reflected in their account. For some young people there were too many rules and they viewed the Hitler Youth leaders as cruel and aggressive.

Interpretation B does show that some young people became less enthusiastic about the Hitler Youth as time went on. Some rebelled and joined groups such as the Edelweiss Pirates and the Swing Youth. However, Interpretation A is more convincing as an account of how most young people responded. The vast majority of young people responded positively to the Hitler Youth and were enthusiastic about what it offered, especially in the first few years of joining up. This enthusiasm may have decreased as time went on, but most young people remained loyal to Hitler, even during the final period of the Second World War.

Revisiting Question 4: How to answer the describe question

Exam Tips: Question 4

- Remind yourself of the key advice for how to answer this type of question on page 16.
- Aim to spend five minutes writing one paragraph.
- Do not simply list the two problems. For each problem, **either** briefly explain why it became a problem **or** give an example of the problem in order to develop your answer.

Practice question	Checklist – What could you include?
Describe two problems faced by Kaiser Wilhelm and his government between 1890 and 1914. (4 marks)	See page 16 for a model answer. • Demands for social reform – growth of trade unions (linked to industrialisation) • Demands for political reforms – Social Democrats, Liberals
Describe two problems for the German government caused by the occupation of the Ruhr in 1923. (4 marks)	• Political criticism – anger and humiliation • Economic problems (Ruhr important industrial area), how to pay for passive resistance (leads to hyperinflation)
Describe two problems that the Weimar government faced as a result of hyperinflation. (4 marks)	• Economic problems – instability, loss of savings, older people who were receiving a pension were affected, food shortages • But – some gained (big business, those with loans) • Political problems, loss of trust in the government, increased opposition

Revisiting Question 5: How to answer the explain question

Exam Tips: Question 5

- Aim to spend about 10 minutes on Question 5 and to write two or three paragraphs. Use the advice on pages 16–17 to help you tackle this type of question.
- Develop your answer by explaining the impact of the changes that took place.
- Demonstrate complex thinking by considering these key questions in your conclusion:
  - Did everyone experience the same impact?
  - How fast did change occur?

Practice question	Checklist – What could you include?
In what ways were the lives of young people affected by Nazi policies between 1933 and 1945? (8 marks)	Paragraph 1 Changes in education: • Curriculum changed to promote Nazi ideas and encourage loyalty to Hitler • Established clear roles for boys and girls Paragraph 2 Changes in life outside of school – Hitler Youth: • Boys taught military skills • Girls prepared for lives as mothers
In what ways were the lives of women affected by Nazi policies between 1933 and 1945? (8 marks)	Paragraph 1 Changes in the role of women: • The 3 Ks, main role to bring up children; restrictions on divorce, abortion and contraception; marriage loans • Lifestyle changes (diet, fashion) Paragraph 2 Economic changes: • Employment restricted – women employed by the state were sacked, no females in the Reichstag, access to university restricted • But – numbers in employment increased during the war
In what ways were the lives of Jewish people affected by Nazi policies between 1933 and 1945? (8 marks)	Paragraph 1 Economic and social changes: • Boycotts of Jewish shops • Jewish people banned from employment (teachers, lawyers, journalists, civil servants) • Nuremberg Laws – citizenship removed Paragraph 2 Physical attacks and the move to the Final Solution: • Kristallnacht • The Wannsee Conference and the establishment of death camps

Revisiting Question 6: How to answer the evaluate question

> **Exam Tips: Question 6**
> - Remember to explain your answer with reference to both bullet points.
> - Aim to spend about 15 minutes on Question 6. Aim to write one paragraph on each of the bullet points, then add a conclusion in which you reach your final judgement on which was the most important.
> - Don't just produce a list of events. For each event, briefly explain why it happened and what happened. Then explain the impact. Don't just say something was important – prove it was!
> - For a top-level mark, you need to show that you are thinking in a complex way about the question. **Use criteria to explain your final judgement.** Why are some causes/developments more important than others? You could think about:
> - What was the **scale** of the impact? How many people were affected?
> - How **long-lasting** was the impact?

Practice question	Checklist – What could you include?
Which of the following was the most important reason why the Weimar Republic was able to recover between 1924 and 1928? • **Economic developments** • **International agreements** (12 marks)	Paragraph 1: • Stopped hyperinflation – introduced the Rentenmark – economic stability returned • Loans from USA (via Dawes Plan) used to invest in the economy – built new factories and houses Paragraph 2: • Paid reparations – which ended occupation of the Ruhr • Locarno Treaties and Kellogg–Brian Pact – rebuilt trust with neighbouring countries • Young Plan – reduced reparations
Which of the following had the greater impact on the German people under Nazi rule? • **Nazi economic policies** • **Nazi social policies** (12 marks)	Paragraph 1: • Reduction in unemployment, Public works schemes, rearmament, RAD • DAF and changes to working conditions Paragraph 2: • Changes in the lives of women • Changes to the churches and in education • Persecution of those who did not fit (Jewish people, mentally ill, those with disabilities)
Which of the following was the most dangerous form of opposition to the Nazi regime? • **Young people** • **Army officers** (12 marks)	Paragraph 1: • White Rose • Swing Youth and Edelweiss Pirates Paragraph 2: • Assassination attempts • 1944 July Bomb Plot
Which of the following was the most important reason why the Nazis were able to control the German people and limit opposition? • **The use of propaganda and censorship** • **The use of repression and the creation of the police state** (12 marks)	Paragraph 1: • Censorship of newspapers, books, art and music • Propaganda via radio, rallies, cinema newsreels Paragraph 2: • Changes in the law – role of judges and the police • SS and concentration camps • Gestapo and system of informers (and block leaders)

Glossary

> **Revision Tip: Test yourself on these definitions**
>
> 1. Cover up the key terms and events – aim to guess the key term/event by reading the definition.
> 2. Cover up the definitions – for each key term/event, aim to give an accurate definition. Then check your answer.

Censorship Stopping people accessing information and ideas that the government does not want them to read, see or hear.

Depression An economic crisis that occurred after the Wall Street Crash. In Germany, it led to high unemployment and poverty.

Enabling Law A law that was passed in 1933, giving Hitler power to act without consulting the Reichstag or the President.

Final Solution The Nazi plan to murder all Jewish people living in Europe.

Führer The German word for leader; Hitler's title after the death of President Hindenburg in 1934.

Gestapo The secret police in Germany.

Hyperinflation Inflation is when money decreases in value, so more is needed to pay for the same things. Hyperinflation is where this gets completely out of hand and prices rise by enormous amounts.

Industrialisation The change that occurs when a country moves from an economy based mainly on agriculture to one based on manufacturing and factories.

July Bomb Plot An attempt made in 1944 by a group of people to kill Hitler, take over the government and end the Second World War.

Kapp Putsch An armed uprising against the government, led by Wolfgang Kapp and involving many Freikorps. It took place in Berlin in 1920.

Munich Putsch An armed uprising that took place in 1923 led by Hitler and the Nazi Party.

Navy Laws Laws passed during the rule of Kaiser Wilhelm II in order to increase the size of the German navy so that it could rival Britain and become a leading world power.

Night of the Long Knives The arrest and murder of Ernst Röhm and other SA leaders on the night of 30 June 1934.

Occupation of the Ruhr The taking over of an area of Germany that was rich in raw materials by French and Belgian troops in 1923.

Police state A country controlled by the police with strict rules over how people can live their lives.

Propaganda Means of spreading political ideas.

Prussian Militarism Admiration for the army and its values – Prussia was the largest state in Germany and many people admired the army in this area.

Public Works Programmes Employment schemes financed by the government to provide jobs, e.g. the Nazis financed the building of autobahns.

Rearmament The Nazi programme to rebuild the strength of the German army. This policy ignored the terms of the Treaty of Versailles that had placed limits on the size of the German army.

Reichstag fire The burning down of the German Parliament in 1933. The Nazis claimed this was the start of a Communist rebellion.

Reparations Compensation for the damage caused by the First World War demanded by the victorious Allies from Germany on the grounds that Germany was to blame for the war.

Self-sufficiency Creating an economy which produces everything that a country needs, meaning that it does not have to trade with other countries.

Socialism Left-wing political movement that believes that resources should be shared out equally and that the government should control the economy.

Trade unions Organisations set up to protect and improve the rights of workers.

White Rose Group A group of students, based in Munich, who protested against Nazi rule.